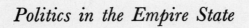

Politics in the Empire State

POLITICS
IN THE
EMPIRE
STATE

Warren Moscow

ALFRED A. KNOPF
NEW YORK
1948

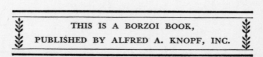

THIS IS A BORZOI BOOK,
PUBLISHED BY ALFRED A. KNOPF, INC.

FIRST EDITION

TO

Jean & Judy

Author's Note

The reader will find this book free of documentation. Instead it is supported by my own experience as a newspaper reporter assigned for more than twenty years to the field of politics and government, local, state, and national. Background material that could not be obtained at the time events occurred was secured afterwards from the primary sources, the politicians themselves. The anecdotes concern either events I witnessed or events recounted directly to me by participants. For my general education as a political reporter, and for assistance in performing that job, I owe a debt to many hundreds of men I have known in politics. In particular I am under obligation for years of wise counsel to James A. Hagerty, senior political reporter for the *New York Times*.

W. M.

CONTENTS

I· IN THE NATION 3

II· THE VOTE-GETTERS 13

III· THE VOTERS 36

IV· WHAT MAKES A PARTY 54

V· THE ELEPHANT 70

VI· THE DONKEY 86

VII· THE SPLINTER PARTIES 102

VIII· THE MACHINES 120

IX· COKE AND BLACKSTONE 148

X· THE LAWMAKERS 166

XI· THE MAN IN THE MANSION 186

XII· ATMOSPHERIC PRESSURE 200

XIII· THE CITIES AND THE STATE 216

XIV· WHO'S GOING TO WIN 225

A CALENDAR OF KEY ELECTIONS IN NEW
YORK STATE, 1918–46 237

INDEX FOLLOWS PAGE 238

Politics in the Empire State

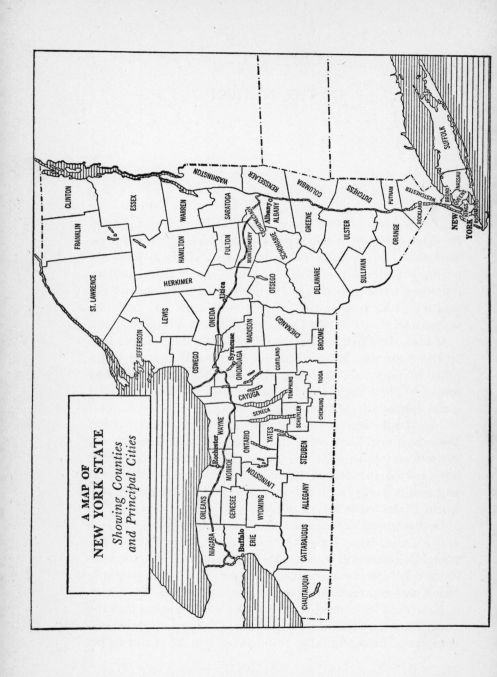

A MAP OF
NEW YORK STATE
*Showing Counties
and Principal Cities*

Chapter I

IN THE NATION

Once upon a time there was a man who was elected President of the United States without having carried New York State. The public, the politicians, and notably the opposing presidential nominee all found it so hard to believe that they went to bed late election night thinking the opposite had happened: that Woodrow Wilson had been defeated and that Charles Evans Hughes was President-elect.

It took days before they could get over their skepticism, and to many the Wilson-Hughes election of 1916 is still a political fairy-tale. It defied all tradition, for Wilson lost not only New York, but all but one of the big industrial states east of the Mississippi, and still carried the electoral college. In the normal course of events, if the West and Far West had not been solid in voting, as they thought, for Wilson and peace, the big Eastern industrial bloc would have settled the occupancy of the White House that year and, incidentally, such things as the trend of domestic and world affairs for at least a decade.

In that group of industrial states, which includes Pennsylvania, Ohio, New Jersey, Massachusetts, Connecticut, Illinois, Michigan, and Indiana, the leader of the flock, the bellwether, is New York State, the largest of them all in population and representation in the electoral college.

New York, of course, is neither the whole nation that too many New Yorkers think it is, nor the unrepresentative collection of "furriners" that bilbos would make it out to be.

3

It has within its borders about a tenth of the nation's population. It is represented in Congress by 45 of the 435 members of the House. It furnished for our two major wars about
a tenth of the membership of our armed forces—the rest
naturally coming from Texas. New York does not consist
entirely of Manhattan Island or even the five boroughs of
New York City, but has boundary waters mingling with
those of Rhode Island and is the last stop before Canada on
countless northern roads.

It has sixty-one urban areas big enough to call themselves
cities, in addition to the one that shares the state's name. It
has potato acreage and duck farms on Long Island, in the
area well to the east of Ebbets Field; it has vast herds of
unpedigreed dairy cattle in the north country along the St.
Lawrence, blooded bulls in Dutchess County, apple orchards
and thoroughbred horses in the central part of the state. It
has Park Avenue and Broadway, slums and slaughterhouses
—in fact, just about a little bit of everything.

So while many think it different from the nation as a
whole, actually it has shown a remarkable capacity for being
influenced politically and governmentally by the same economic, social, and religious forces that figure importantly
in any state where there is a division between urban and
rural populations, where one big city would dominate the
government except that the rest of the state won't let it.

To politicians, the fact that New York is representative of
and similar to so many other industrial states becomes an
important reason, at least once every four years, for taking
New York to their bosom. The man who carries New York
starts out with a bloc of 47 of the 266 electoral votes needed
to win control of the White House, and by experience the
politicians also know that the man who carries New York
carries the nation.

It is natural that New York, as principal center of the nation's wealth, as the Mecca of financial success or recognition

in so many fields, should furnish a large share of the nation's political leadership. Its tendency in that direction is further increased by the desire of the politicians in the nation to name for the Presidency a man who can win, which to them means a man who can carry New York.

Thus in the twenty presidential elections from the end of the Civil War through 1944 there have been fourteen campaigns in which at least one of the principal nominees was a New Yorker. In two of them both major-party nominees called New York home. Look over the list. There was Horatio Seymour and then Horace Greeley in the first two elections after the death of Lincoln. Next came Tilden, who carried New York and the nation, but was counted out by an electoral commission. Cleveland ran three times. There were Teddy Roosevelt and Alton B. Parker in 1904, with T. R. again as a Progressive in 1912.

Then came Hughes and Al Smith, Franklin Roosevelt four elections in a row, with Tom Dewey as his opponent in F. D. R.'s last campaign. In this tabulation Dewey is counted as a New Yorker despite his Michigan birth and upbringing, because his entire public career has been in New York; but the totals do not include John W. Davis of the 1924 campaign and Wendell L. Willkie of 1940, two adopted sons whose ties of nativity to West Virginia and Indiana respectively were revived during campaign time to take the curse off the direct Wall Street connections they had—Davis as lawyer for the House of Morgan and Willkie as head of a big utility company. They were the only two direct Wall Street nominees.

All of the others but Greeley and Parker had previously been elected Governor of New York; they had shown their parties the vote-getting strength that seemed to justify the conclusion that if nominated for the Presidency, they would have at least an even chance of adding to their party's column the state's cherished electoral votes. What it amounts to is that every Governor of New York is ex-officio a potential presidential nominee unless barred constitutionally by foreign birth or practically by racial or religious consideration.

For example, Franklin D. Roosevelt had been Governor of New York for exactly five months when the annual conference of Governors met in New London, Connecticut, in June 1929. He had not had the time to show his capacity or talent for leadership; but to observers at that conference there was no mistaking the appraising glances of some thirty other Governors. Roosevelt had, of course, the attraction of his name, which shone then with the luster of the earlier Roosevelt. But they looked him over closely, then and there, because he held the Governorship of New York, which had become a recognized stepping-stone to the nomination for the White House.

Politicians operating with New York as a home base have a priceless, unpurchasable advantage over their competitors. They do their stuff in front of enormous publicity mirrors that reflect their actions all over the nation. Everyone knows there are many persons who do not like New York and the New York influence and feel the same distaste for people they regard as typical New Yorkers, but the nation's editors also know that there are very few who are not interested in what goes on in New York. Its fashions, its murders, its sex life, and its politics get space day in and day out, week in and week out, in the newspapers of the other big cities around the country, in the small-town journals, in the magazines of national circulation. With that free advertising, New York's politicians achieve their national reputations, for better or for worse.

Dewey is an example. His name and his picture have been in every paper and every magazine in the country over a period of a dozen years. In his early twenties he left his home town of Owosso, Michigan, to study singing and then practice law in New York. If by chance he had gone instead to near-by Detroit and as a public prosecuter had sent that city's well-known Purple Gang to jail, instead of working on Jimmy Hines and Lucky Luciano, would he have gone so far? Would he have been able to enter national politics at the tender age of thirty-eight as he did in 1940 when he went to the Philadelphia national convention with more delegates pledged to him for the Presidency than any other contender? His most ardent admirers would not argue the point.

When Thomas Nast drew his famous cartoon of Tammany in prison stripes, back in the days of Boss Tweed, he dramatized New York politics for the nation. The old Pendergast crowd in Midwestern Kansas City used tactics that make Tammany at its worst look like an organization of political reformers; Indiana has always had machines of both parties operating with brazen effrontery; it was Frank Hague, in Jersey City, not any Tammany boss, who proclaimed: "I am the law." But it will always be Tammany that typifies the machine type of government in the eyes of many people, and there will always be men making national reputations by having fought and beaten it. By now Tammany has been beaten so often that instead of being a predatory tiger cat, it is much more like a skinned, striped hearth rug.

It has not had control of the state for years, and in the city it is outvoted by the organization in Brooklyn and outmaneuvered by the machine in the Bronx. But the legend lingers on. Such is the power of the pen, the well-drawn cartoon, and the impact of a picturesque name.

Not all of New York's political eminence can be attributed to Tammany's disrepute, to the fame and notoriety achieved by its leaders. The state has earned a great deal of its national political prestige by its leadership in governmental trends. There are those who will argue that Wisconsin, under the leadership of old Bob La Follette, set the pace for state governments during the twentieth century. Wisconsin did have great influence, but so did New York, and there is not much point in arguing about which influence was the greater.

One of the outstanding trends of the current century, blooming early in both states, was the growth of government activities. It stemmed from a demand for regulation, for collective security, to make sure that a complex industrial applecart was not kicked over by a greedy few. There will be some who will interpret collective security as Communism. It has not meant that in New York. The state has the largest collection of Communists in the country, but they number only about 50,000 party members out of more than 6,000,000 voters, and long before they figured in the state's politics, the demand for "regulation" was heard.

I will not attempt to draw the line where regulation and collective security end and Communism begins, but politicians regard it as a truism that everyone, including the most rugged individualist, desires regulation of some kind for the other fellow. The farmers in the West forced the first move nationally with their demand for regulation of railroad freight rates and they have clamored consistently for the breaking up of farm-machinery trusts. The small businessman in the East wants regulation of the public utility that gives him his light and his power, and the laboring man wants a ceiling on the prices of what he buys.

This trend was felt in New York State, in the daily workings of the state government, earlier than in most places and long before price ceilings or commodity and business controls were thought to be within the power of the federal government. It has had the most effective, though still imperfect, public-utility regulation of any state in the Union; it was a leader in setting up factory inspection and tenement-house laws, in fixing mandatory workmen's compensation for injuries. These things led inevitably to big government in New York before it was established in the nation. It may be noted that the national government achieved its great size during the thirteen years of the New Deal, headed by a New Yorker as President and administered to a large degree by New Yorkers in cabinet posts and at the head of big new governmental agencies.

The scope of government in New York compared with that in some other states was impressed in simple, visible form upon me when I was in Topeka in 1936 covering the presidential campaign of Alf M. Landon, Governor of Kansas. Landon had been nominated that year by the Republicans with the campaign slogan that he had balanced his budget, in comparison with the debt being piled up in Washington. Landon, a charming gentleman of considerable capacity, was in charge of a state government that spent, in its total annual budget, exactly the same sum that New York City was spending that year for fixing holes in its truck-pounded streets. And another item: in New York, ten years before the Landon campaign, the people had voted to bond the state up to $300,000,000 to get collective protection against railroad grade-crossing dangers, to build over- and under-passes at all main intersections; but in 1936 the Union Pacific Railroad still sent its streamliners whizzing across the main street of the Kansas state capital at grade, with only a watchman waving a flag to guard the crossing. In any number of similar ways—the fact, for instance, that two state departments were housed in one small room in the Capital—Kansas represented small, decentralized government, with the basic power resting in its hundred-odd county seats, in contrast to the New York type of centralized authority. Whatever the trend may be in the future, the people of the nation that year rejected the Kansas concept— with only Maine and Vermont dissenting—and voted for Roosevelt's New York style of democracy.

9

But Roosevelt, even though he brought to the White House a breadth of vision and a daring rare among men, should not be given either the credit or the blame for New York's type and theory of government. He was an inheritor rather than an originator. Long before he went to Washington, many years before he became Governor, the need for economic reform through government supervision had been dramatized for New Yorkers by the famous Triangle Shirtwaist Company fire of 1911. Scores of girls working in that sweatshop were burned to death or killed leaping from the flaming building in which they had been trapped. The Triangle Company occupied a rat-hole, but it was then a typical city factory.

The disaster roused the social consciousness of the people and of the politicians, and the cause of reform was taken up by men like Al Smith, Bob Wagner, Jimmy Walker, and Jim Foley. Frances Perkins, in her reminiscenses of Roosevelt, tells how Charles Francis Murphy, leader of Tammany Hall, became a convert, too. Miss Perkins, then a young and ardent social worker, had managed to slip through the Legislature a bill limiting factory employment of women to fifty-four hours a week. Murphy told her he had been opposed to the measure, but "it made a lot of votes for us," and he was for it and others like it from then on.

That was in 1912, and for a dozen years, as long as Murphy lived, Smith, Wagner, and their associates were assured of the political support that was all-important, for Murphy's word was law in those days. Smith, taking the issues to the people, was particularly effective in making them understand how government could be made to work in their behalf.

Smith fought not only for improved working conditions, but for public water-power ownership, for preservation of the wild forest lands and the building of new parks and beaches, to preserve what he regarded as common property

for the benefit of all rather than the few. In the same way
that Roosevelt left his indelible mark on the structure and
history of the nation, Smith left his on the state. Up to his
eight-year regime as Governor the state government was a
loose collection of bureaus and agencies—nobody knew exactly how many—and efficient administration of the greatly
increased powers Smith urged for the state would have been
impossible. With the approval of the people, by constitutional amendments, he wrapped up the odds and ends into
a dozen and a half state departments, centralized and powerful. It was the most thorough renovation of a state government the nation had seen until then.

Many voters today remember Smith only as a man who
tied up with a millionaires' coalition in 1936, under the
title of the Liberty League, to try to beat Roosevelt, who
had taken the presidential nomination away from him four
years before. That was a different Smith, a man who happened to leave public office a few years too soon, disappointed because he failed to achieve the Presidency and
definitely dated in his views. Those with longer memories
and better perspective know that Smith, more than any
other one man, set the tone for the government the people
get in New York State, and that politicians of both parties
still run on his record.

New York has had good government and bad, ranging
from the corruption of Tweed to the social consciousness of
Smith and his successors. It has shown how it could be both
radical and conservative, sending a Vito Marcantonio and a
John Taber to the same Congress at the same election. Population shifts have caused changes in voting habits, so that
Brooklyn, which once used to furnish the Republicans at
least a partial offset to Tammany's strength in Manhattan,
became the strongest Democratic voting unit in the nation.
The state, in comparison with the one-party states of the
South and the two-party system that exists elsewhere, has

found room in its political spectrum for not one, but two actively functioning minor parties, big enough to be factors in determining an election. This comes about because in New York, even after recently imposed limitations, it has been possible for minor parties to nominate the same candidate as one of the major parties, and to have its votes counted for that candidate in the election totals.

Despite this, there is less chance for a political mugwump to get places in New York than there is elsewhere. New York sees no goat-gland doctor coming close to election as governor because of the panaceas he purveys by radio. No hillbilly bands or biscuit-passers threaten the established political order. New York's voters are tied more closely to the state's recognized political parties than is the general rule elsewhere, and only the regularly nominated candidates figure importantly in the election results. The Democratic and Republican parties have taken turns as the dominant party in the state. The American Labor and Liberal parties, one formed in 1936 and the other in 1944, can contribute to the success or defeat of either major party by alliance with one or the other or by taking independent action, but neither the ALP, the Liberals, nor any other independent group can come close to electing a candidate for high public office on a state-wide basis.

Both major parties have developed a sense of state-wide responsibility. They know they have to run their candidates in Yonkers as well as Penn Yan, in Syracuse as well as Canarsie. The result is a democracy calculated to do the most good for and secure the most votes of the greatest number of people.

Chapter II

THE VOTE-GETTERS

In every state, at one time or another, there has appeared some outstanding political figure to dominate the scene, to win election after election for himself or for his followers. There was Norris of Nebraska, Borah of Idaho, and Huey Long of Louisiana, who promised to make every man a king. All were national figures while they lived, as well as powers on their home playing fields.

In New York State, blessed as it is with so much of the nation's wealth, there has been a plethora of outstanding men. Probably during his time as Governor the biggest of all in the minds and the hearts of the home-state voters was Al Smith. But his period has long gone by, and in the last decade there have been at least four other men who shared in varying degrees the power and the glory.

The backgrounds of Franklin D. Roosevelt, Herbert H. Lehman, Fiorello H. La Guardia, and Thomas E. Dewey were as different as their political philosophies, representing as they did landed aristocracy, high finance, the city streets, and the small town. The first two were Democrats, La Guardia a "mugwump," and Dewey, of course, an organization Republican. Because they were so different, it seems pertinent to try to explain, briefly, how each rose to high public office and how, once there, he held the fealty of the voters.

ROOSEVELT

Franklin D. Roosevelt was always a firm believer in his own destiny, in his "lucky star." There always may be some disagreement on the true measure of Roosevelt's greatness, but there should be none on his own premise that it took a remarkable series of events, beyond his own control, to pave his way to the Presidency.

The first of these was the election, in 1910, of this tall, handsome, young Democrat to the state Senate from the normally Republican Hudson River Valley district in which he lived. His family was well known, but that could not have elected him, nor could anything else if the Republican Party had not at that time been in the process of splitting into two camps—the Old Guard followers of William Howard Taft, and the Progressive supporters of Franklin's own distant cousin Theodore Roosevelt.

Franklin Roosevelt, in his first Senate term, took on Tammany Hall as an opponent, successfully leading a legislative revolt that defeated Charles F. Murphy's choice for United States senator. The Legislature, which elected senators in those days, deadlocked for months and finally picked a compromise candidate acceptable to Roosevelt. It was a victory for the young Dutchess County Democrat, but he seemed "through" politically in the state, for it was thought no one could buck Murphy within the Democratic Party and get away with it.

But at the Baltimore national convention of 1912 Murphy made one of his rare mistakes. He backed Champ Clark for the Democratic presidential nomination against Woodrow Wilson, and it was Wilson who was nominated and elected.

Wilson refused to recognize Murphy in the distribution of federal patronage and, as a definite anti-Tammany gesture, picked Roosevelt out of the state of New York and put him in his official family in Washington as Assistant Secretary of the Navy. That service in Washington for eight years led to Roosevelt's projection into national politics in 1920 as the Democratic vice-presidential nominee, and even though the Cox-Roosevelt ticket was snowed under that year, the experience proved invaluable later.

His third major break came in 1928 when Al Smith, running for President, asked Roosevelt to be the candidate for governor of New York. Smith felt he needed Roosevelt, a prominent Protestant, to give political "balance" to the ticket in New York State, headed as it was by Smith, a Catholic, and with a Jew, Herbert H. Lehman, the scheduled nominee for lieutenant governor. Roosevelt declined.

He argued that if he had four more years in which to enjoy the curative waters at Warm Springs, Georgia, he might recover some use of his legs, crippled by paralysis since 1921. There was unquestioned sincerity and validity behind that argument. However, the late Louis McHenry Howe, who was Roosevelt's confidant, leg-man, and secretary for twenty-five years, once told me that there was another reason besides his health for Roosevelt's refusal to run for governor in 1928. Both he and Howe figured it was "too early" on the political timetable.

Crippled though he was, Roosevelt had always looked forward to being president some day. He had spent his years in bed writing or dictating letters, corresponding with the men he had met in the 1920 campaign, and keeping himself informed about conditions in every part of the nation, all with a purpose in mind. He had the time element figured out, too. He reasoned, Howe said, that the Republicans were due to win the national election with Hoover in 1928 and would probably be able to hold the office for two terms, until 1936. So if Roosevelt ran for governor of New York in 1932 instead of 1928, he would be in the presidential picture at the proper time.

But Smith's pleas overrode Roosevelt's sense of timing as well as his concern about his health, and Roosevelt fortunately yielded. The turn in the national tide Roosevelt had predicted for 1936 came instead in 1932, owing to the stock-market crash and the depression, and Roosevelt, with four years behind him then as Governor of New York, was the natural nominee of his party.

The next remarkable circumstance in the Roosevelt story was that Smith, idol of New York, failed to carry the state for the Presidency, losing it by 111,000 votes, while Roosevelt, who by no means approached Smith in political stature at that time, carried it by 26,000, the smallest margin in a decade. Roosevelt, too, would have lost had it not been for a political deal made up-state. Without being a party to it, he was the principal beneficiary.

The Republican candidate for governor that year, opposing Roosevelt, was Albert Ottinger, a capable Attorney General of the state, popular with the public but unfortunately endowed with the Napoleonic complex that afflicts some short men. Early in the campaign, by exhibitions of self-importance, Ottinger managed to snub or offend most of his Republican running-mates. Hamilton Ward, of Erie, seeking to succeed Ottinger as attorney general, was one of these.

Ward's friends in Erie are credited with having made an agreement with the Democrats there under which votes for Ward for attorney general were swapped for votes for Roosevelt for governor. Incidentally Ward was also elected. Roosevelt received more votes than Smith in Erie, though he was running for lesser office, and Ward received 20,000 more votes than Ottinger. Ottinger ran far enough behind his ticket in the western section of the state to lose the Governorship. Had he had a more cordial attitude toward his running-mates, Roosevelt would have been beaten and the latter's chances for being nominated for the Presidency in 1932 would have been negligible, almost nonexistent.

The whole trend of world affairs might easily have been different. Instead, the New Deal was conceived and carried into operation; America stayed under Roosevelt's leadership to become the arsenal of democracy and the greatest military power on earth; the domestic economy underwent the most drastic revision since the nation was founded; and the name of Roosevelt, elected four times, gained a place in history alongside those of Lincoln, Jefferson, and Washington.

Roosevelt took few political gambles during the four years he held the Governorship, never forgetting his White House goal. In general he showed none of the daring he demonstrated later as President, and there were undoubtedly many in New York who shared Walter Lippmann's appraisal, printed at the time, of Roosevelt as an amiable man with no particular qualifications for the Presidency.

Roosevelt had been re-elected Governor in 1930 by the then record margin of 725,000 votes, which was less a tribute to his personality and record than a reflection of growing dissatisfaction with the Hoover administration in the nation. But to his own national party it marked Roosevelt as a Democrat who could carry New York and therefore could probably be elected president. From then on he never left the national limelight. He cemented his hold on the voters of his home state after, rather than before, he was sworn in as President on that grim 4th of March in 1933.

At the time, the economic plight of the nation showed itself at its worst in New York City and state. The government of the big city was bankrupt, and so were many of its great industries. The luxury trades and foreign commerce, which customarily furnished a living to so many of its people, had been the first victims of the depression and by 1933 had been dead for more than three years.

People lost their savings in bank failures and in the Wall Street crash. They lost their jobs, and their homes. Financial institutions that had not failed retained theoretical solvency by foreclosing inflated mortgages. There was no system of public relief, and apple-selling on street corners became the vogue.

The story of how F. D. R. captured the imagination of the people of the nation by his quick remedial steps has been told many times; it need not be repeated here. But it should be pointed out that while in some parts of the country some of his reforms lost popularity, they never did in New York. In his home state, bank-deposit insurance, the home and work relief programs, the social-security legislation, the Home Owners' Loan Corporation, the establishment of a Securities and Exchange Commission, all were good for votes as long as he continued running for office. The smallest majority Roosevelt ever received in New York, after his original election as Governor in 1928 was the 224,-000 by which he defeated Wendell L. Willkie in 1940. In most states that would be called a landslide.

Roosevelt played opportunistic politics with a nonchalance and a flair not seen in the White House since the days of T. R. and Lincoln, but the New York public always seemed to have forgiveness in its heart. All the world loves a good performance, and Roosevelt never gave a bad one. There was magic in his manner, and his calm, resonant voice emanating from the White House in his fireside chats told the millions in the cities that all was right with the world, or that he would soon help make it so. They believed in him as a leader, approved his policies, and paid no heed to criticism of him.

His opposition to Hitlerism, his wartime leadership, his standing as a world figure who might bring permanent peace—all were tremendous political assets in his home state.

His greatest personal triumph in New York came in the twilight of his years, on a bitter October day in 1944. He was touring New York City, to prove to the voters he was well enough to carry on as President for another four years.

The king was showing himself to his loyal subjects, to down ill-founded but widespread rumors. Rain poured from leaden skies, a biting wind chilled those foolhardy enough to venture out. But there were millions who deemed it necessary. They waved rain-soaked arms at Roosevelt in an open car and cheered from throats that soon would be sore. The people saw him and believed him as they always had.

LEHMAN

Herbert H. Lehman was never a professional politician. He did not at any early age embark on a political or governmental career, and when he first ran for public office, it was somebody else's idea. Yet his name became as standard on the ballot as the major-party emblems, the eagle and the star. Only the tradition that no man of his religious faith could ever be a candidate for the Presidency kept him from being a definite possibility for the highest office in the land.

In the middle twenties he was the head of the wealthy private banking firm of Lehman Brothers. He was active in philanthropic and social work, which brought him into contact with Al Smith, then Governor. Smith admired him and he admired Smith. Lehman showed his approval of Smith in a practical way. In support of Smith's campaigns for re-election in 1924 and 1926 Lehman contributed liberally, and in the pre-convention and presidential campaigns of 1928 he gave the almost incredibly large sum of $500,000 to aid Smith's ambitions.

There has never been any indication that Lehman at that time even thought of any political reward. He believed in Smith and he could spare the money. But it was natural for Smith, in September of that year, seeking the political balance of the ticket mentioned in connection with Roosevelt's selection for the Governorship, to pick for the "Jewish spot" the man who believed in his policies and was his friend. Lehman had at least as great prestige among members of his own faith as any man ever nominated by a major party for state-wide office. His record, his background, his beliefs were all impeccable. He was elected Lieutenant Governor with ease, though Roosevelt only squeaked through and Smith himself was defeated.

Lehman moved out of his Park Avenue suite and into a couple of Albany hotel rooms to devote his full time and talents to a job—the Lieutenant-Governorship—which up to then had always been regarded as a political sinecure. He stayed on that job so faithfully that Roosevelt was able, while Governor, to tour the country in behalf of his own presidential ambitions and also, for his health, to relax at Warm Springs, knowing that the trusty Lehman was Acting Governor. F. D. R. called him his "good right arm."

They differed on an important matter only once, years later, when Roosevelt tried to "pack" the United States Supreme Court. Lehman, undoubtedly convinced by his brother Irving, associate and later chief judge of the state Court of Appeals, came out publicly against the plan. It dealt the measure, then pending in the Senate, a staggering blow, and the Roosevelt-Lehman relationship suffered for a short time.

But back in 1932 Roosevelt, just nominated for the Presidency, was determined that Lehman should be his successor as governor. Tammany, still in control in New York, had fought Roosevelt's nomination for the Presidency and had lost. It had seen him prepared to remove Walker as Mayor. It was all the more determined to get at least the Governorship under its control. Allied with an up-state bloc of county leaders, Tammany appeared to have the votes in the nominating convention to beat Lehman.

But Roosevelt, arriving in Albany from a campaign tour, served notice he would speak from the convention-hall platform for Lehman's nomination, putting behind his demand all his prestige as the party's national nominee for president, with almost a certainty of election. "I'll see you at the convention hall," Roosevelt told John F. Curry, the Tammany leader, over the telephone from the executive mansion.

And Smith, disappointed as he was that year in not getting a second crack at the Presidency, put all pique aside and threw his very important state prestige behind Lehman, though Lehman was a Roosevelt supporter at the party's national convention. He did it in typical Smith fashion. Leaning across the table in the traditionally smoke-filled conference room, he told Curry that unless he nominated Lehman for governor, he himself would take control of New York City away from Curry the following year by running for mayor.

"On what ticket?" Curry sneered.

"On a Chinese laundry ticket I can beat you and your crowd," Smith retorted.

Curry knew Al meant what he said. An hour before the balloting was to start he gave in. Lehman was nominated and later elected Governor. He was re-elected in 1934, in 1936, and again in 1938, the last time for a newly lengthened term of four years. All told, he served four years as Lieutenant Governor and Acting Governor and ten years as Governor. He was defeated for public office only once, in the Republican landslide of 1946, when he returned to state politics as his party's nominee for United States senator. He ran more than 400,000 votes ahead of his ticket, but the trend that year was too much for even Herbert Lehman to overcome. It is worth noting that even in that campaign, he fared better up-state as well as down than the head of his party's ticket, though his own Republican opponent was an up-state man.

What was remarkable about Lehman was that he seemed to be about as colorless a candidate as any party could present. He was a thorough gentleman, but not a rousing campaigner. Short in build and nervous in manner, he was never able to put drama into statistics the way Smith could. He had none of Roosevelt's forensic tricks with which to captivate an audience. He had too much personal dignity to put on a show like La Guardia. Nor was he a trained, made, speech-maker like Dewey.

What convinced the people was that same utter lack of color, his obvious sincerity of purpose, and his solidity as a citizen. He had, naturally, the support of voters of his own religious faith, but in every one of his campaigns, even that of 1946, there were Republican businessmen and bankers, even farmers, of entirely different political and religious creeds, who voted for Lehman because they were convinced that he was the best man available for the job at the time. Students of state government in general are convinced that his administration of New York State was outstanding.

The issue of anti-Semitism operated against Lehman only once. This was in 1938 when Dewey ran for governor for the first time. It should be said in fairness to Dewey that he did not raise the issue, but he happened to be the first Protestant nominated for the Governorship by his party in nearly a decade, and in up-state sections the desire of the people to vote for "one of our own" was translated shortly into a more active resistance to Lehman's re-election. For a time it seemed likely to defeat Lehman, but Republican Jews in New York City left their party en masse when they realized what was happening. Those who question this need only look at the figures, which show that Dewey carried up-state by 619,000, a figure normally high enough to ensure election, but the Lehman forces rallied a majority of 683,-000 in New York City.

His record as Governor was a fine one. Its motivation was consistently good, and the office-holders he selected were, in the main, experts in their fields. He inherited a hundred-million-dollar deficit from Roosevelt and by careful nursing of the pennies, plus increased state revenues, had turned the deficit into an equally large surplus when he left office. He stressed public-utility regulation, public low-cost housing, and relief for the needy and generally gave to the state a "little New Deal." His administration, however, was free of the looseness that sometimes brought criticism on the administration in Washington, and Lehman therefore was never subjected to the charges of "radicalism." The people wouldn't have believed them of a banker, anyhow.

If Lehman had any weakness, it was his lack of a sense of humor, his ever present dead seriousness. The robes of office wore heavily on him. He felt that there was required of a public official a dignity greater than that demanded of any private citizen, no matter how highly placed.

The night he left office, after ten years as Governor, the legislative correspondents in Albany gave him a private party attended only by the retiring Governor and about a dozen newspapermen. It was held in the home of a veteran correspondent. Lehman was free of the cares of office, and he really relaxed and talked more freely than usual of his life in Albany. He confessed that all the time he had been Governor he had had a desire to eat in Keeler's, Albany's deservedly famous and traditional eating-place. But he never had. He thought it was somehow unbecoming for the Governor to be seen eating in a public restaurant.

LA GUARDIA

Fiorello H. La Guardia, before he became Mayor of New York City, was one of the best Representatives ever to sit in Congress. He studied legislation, he knew the details of every bill he voted on, and he had a remarkable comprehension of the issues of the day. He had the complete respect of his fellows; he worked hard for the people of the districts he represented. He was elected at different times from two of them, and he unquestionably represented their political beliefs. He championed labor and fought for the under dog when few others thought that expedient.

As Mayor he was equally hard-working. He knew the problems of his city, he worked at them, and his record when he quit office was by far the best in the history of the Greater City. He would not stand for the waste of a city dollar, nor would he allow a favor to be purchased. The city he left behind him is far and away his best memorial. Yet if he missed real greatness, of which he was capable, it was because of emotional instability. And those who forgave him for this were still confronted with his broad streak of political opportunism.

For example, his constant theme in campaigns from 1933 onward was that he would keep the "clubhouse loafers" off the political payroll, that professional politicians were "bums" with whom he would not associate. But only four years before, when he ran unsuccessfully for mayor against Jimmy Walker, he told the Republican city convention that nominated him that when he was elected, the jobs would go to the delegates—the same clubhouse loafers and bums— present at that nominating convention. This was not a change of heart in La Guardia, simply a change of times.

By 1933, the year he was elected Mayor for the first time, clean, nonpartisan city government was a crying need and La Guardia was willing to be the man of the hour. Still he almost missed gaining the nomination; and nomination that year virtually meant election because of the Democratic tin-box scandals unveiled by the Seabury investigation, plus the city's bankruptcy, and the failure of John P. O'Brien, Walker's interim successor, to show any qualifications for the job of cleaning out truly Augean stables.

La Guardia's record as a political maverick was too well

known for some of the respectable and conservative people in the reform movement to be enthusiastic about him. The Republican party organization was less so, and the independent committee of reformers that was picking the ticket to oust Tammany actually announced its selection of John F. O'Ryan, a National Guard commander with a record in the first World War.

The Republicans were also about to accept O'Ryan, a step that would have left La Guardia completely out of the picture. But Seabury, convinced of La Guardia's innate incorruptibility, insisted on his selection, and W. Kingsland Macy, the Republican state chairman, by hook or by crook swung enough Republican committee votes to La Guardia to cinch the nomination. It was perhaps typical of La Guardia's mental processes that while he kept a commitment to make O'Ryan Police Commissioner in return for the latter's withdrawal from the mayoralty picture, he turned his political fire on Macy at the earliest possible opportunity. He did not want any politician, even the one who had made him Mayor, to think he felt under political obligation to him.

La Guardia as Mayor squeezed a great deal of water out of the city budget. While expenses did not go down, he gave the city many things it had paid for but did not get from previous administrations. Parks were refurbished, new ones were created. Playgrounds and swimming-pools were built in the slums; plans for arterial highways and subway extensions, which had been kicking around for years, were carried out. The land-condemnation racket, which milked the city treasury for the benefit of favored lawyers, land-owners, and politicians in connection with city improvements, was ended.

Possibly his greatest achievement was making a bankrupt city solvent. La Guardia restored the city financially and morally. When he took over, the bankers were doling out loans in small sums, just enough at one time to prevent default on city obligations. Otherwise the city's credit was gone. La Guardia had the courage to face reality, and though he had always fought a sales tax in Congress, he enacted a sales tax in New York to give the city a source of revenue beyond the lagging real-estate levies. The tax he sponsored was the best-drawn sales tax in the nation; it has been copied in many places, and in New York its form has never been substantially changed.

Another problem was the morale of city employees. They had none. That Mayor Jimmy Walker did not go to work until three in the afternoon, or later, and that favors could be bought in almost any city department from men at or near the top, were known to the rank and file, and their work suffered. La Guardia brought in genuine career men as administrators. He demanded a day's work for a day's pay. He made money-honesty a fetish.

The memory of the city's condition before he took it over was kept fresh in the minds of the voters by La Guardia in his speeches during campaigns and in his regular weekly radio talks. It served to re-elect him in 1937 and again in 1941. New Yorkers liked the government he gave them and believed his declarations that if he were defeated, the "same old gang" would come back in control. He won, too, a sort of amused affection from the people by his constant chasing after fire-engines, his rushing everywhere in a hurry. They liked his "little boy with a big hat" personality.

He was quick to explode, and the stories of his blow-ups are legion. In a fit of temper one day he ordered two competent city officials fired. He told their superior to have the resignations on his desk by ten o'clock the next morning, or else. The victims, feeling aggrieved, did not comply with his demand, and when noon had passed the next day without further word from the Mayor, the two officials left their offices and got drunk, ducking the retribution they were sure would come in some terrible and swift form. They never heard from the Mayor again. That is, until six months later, when he promoted them.

Another time he fired a secretary of whom he was very fond, after a violent quarrel that wound up with the secretary calling the Mayor a "no-good guinea ——" and a "dago ——." La Guardia tearfully explained later that he didn't mind being called a —— and a ——, but why did the secretary have to inject the race issue? He asked the secretary to return to work, and it was not his fault that the latter, equally temperamental, refused.

At another period it was Robert Moses, New York's Master Builder, who was always threatening to resign from one of his numerous posts. Fiorello got tired of it, and the next time Moses came in and threatened to quit, La Guardia gave him a pad of printed forms, reading: "I, Robert Moses, hereby resign as . . . . effective . . . ." Moses heaved the forms into the waste-basket— exactly what he was supposed to do.

Politically La Guardia always played on the New Deal team. Possibly because it helped him get federal funds for the rebuilding of New York—much more likely because he was ideologically close—he was a continued supporter of Roosevelt in national affairs. Though he was elected Mayor three times on the Republican ticket, he never supported a Republican candidate for top state or national office. The closest he came was in 1938, when he privately promised to be Tom Dewey's New York City campaign manager, but he never carried this through and he wound up by coming out for Lehman two days before election. Roosevelt was fond of La Guardia, and the President's known friendship was an asset to La Guardia in municipal campaigns and a constant irritation to the Democratic city machines.

Fiorello always dreamed of national political office, of returning to his beloved Washington as United States senator or as vice president. He hoped that the directorship of civilian defense, which he undertook in 1942, would help him toward his goal, but he failed in that job and never really recovered from the disappointment. Franklin Roosevelt promised, and actually tried, to appoint La Guardia a general in the army, in the military government branch, but Henry L. Stimson and George C. Marshall would not stand for it, and the appointment never got past Marshall's desk. With one disappointment or another, and failing health, his last years as Mayor were filled with bitterness and did not match in brilliance his early administrations.

La Guardia put on, for public consumption, the attitude that he was retiring from the mayoralty of his own free will in 1945. There is reason to believe otherwise. The office represented his only chance to stay in the political picture. But he was afraid, probably with reason, that the public had by then become so accustomed to the reforms he had initiated that he would not be re-elected. Also he knew that the Republicans were determined, once and for all, that he should not have their nomination.

The newly formed Liberal Party, headed by right-wing labor leaders who had always backed him before, was against him this time. He had insulted their leaders, needlessly and heedlessly, once too often, in those fits of temper that kept him from true greatness. So when the Liberals and the Republicans united on Jonah J. Goldstein as a candidate for mayor, La Guardia made sure that the men who had turned him down would not win with their new choice. He induced Newbold Morris, a close political associate, to enter the race on a third ticket, doubly ensuring the election of O'Dwyer. The city got O'Dwyer as Mayor, and it was probably the best tribute ever given La Guardia that O'Dwyer started off trying to follow in the La Guardia tradition of clean, constructive government. The city truly mourned

La Guardia when he died, and it will long remember his administrations.

DEWEY

When Tom Dewey ran for district attorney of New York County in 1937, there were signs posted in a number of polling places in Brooklyn that read: "Dewey is not running in this county." Harassed election officials knew of no other way of convincing hundreds of voters that they were not being deprived of a part of their franchise right. Probably no other purely local candidate ever excited such interest among the voters as did Dewey, then just thirty-five years old, fresh from the cleaning up of Manhattan's rackets. His name had been in screaming headlines almost every day of the two years that he had been special prosecutor. A word about the rackets.

The repeal of prohibition had taken away the source of easy living from a bunch of hoodlums who had never earned a dollar at honest work. They knew how to use brass knuckles and guns. Adding knowledge of how to use kerosene or acids to spoil quantities of food or clothing, they formed "protective associations," and any merchant who was willing to pay ten or fifteen dollars a week was "protected" against being beaten, shot, or having his stock of merchandise ruined by the same crew. The tribute ran into millions of dollars annually and the gangs were run by higher-ups who had close alliances with certain Tammany district leaders. The latter gave them immunity from arrest or prosecution year round in return for cash and work at the polls at the primaries or on election day. They were safe as long as the prosecutor's office and the police department were in the hands of their political friends.

But a county grand jury "ran away" from its controlled prosecutor's staff, and the foreman appealed to the Governor to give it the powers to do something about the rackets. Lehman was Governor, and in line with his rule—not followed by Dewey—that special prosecutors be named from those of the opposing political faith, he offered to appoint any one of three prominent Republican lawyers to carry on a thorough probe. He made his offer through the influential Association of the Bar of the City of New York. George Z. Medalie, who had picked up Dewey five years before as a "bright young man," was then a power in the Bar Association and, with faith in Dewey, he prevailed on all of the Governor's nominees to decline and to join him in suggesting Dewey instead. Lehman hesitated, not for partisan reasons or because Dewey at the time looked like a future political menace, but because of Dewey's youth and relative inexperience. But he appointed him anyhow.

For two years Dewey did an outstanding job. He handpicked his staff of assistants; he laid down rules so firmly that patrolmen and investigators working out of his office knew they would be cashiered if they were responsible for the slightest leak. He established headquarters in a big office building where witnesses could come and go without easy identification. He had the imagination to see that if protection in fact, not theory, was given to complaining witnesses—if they could be sure that the racketeers would be behind bars the next day, instead of waiting to beat them up—the rackets could be broken.

He made legal history by getting from the Governor and the Legislature special conspiracy laws, permitting conviction of a group on evidence that only linked them one by one to established parts of the crime. He secured plenty of convictions by using special "blue ribbon" panels of jurors with high standing in the community and presumably more than average intelligence. Many witnesses lived in secret hide-outs at county expense for months, until the chain of evidence was complete, but it was worth it to the people and no one got far with complaints about the methods Dewey used.

He was "Mr. District Attorney" with all the same bristling drama of the later radio presentations. He dealt in pimps, gunmen, and madams whose very names, like Cokey Flo or Charley Lucky, made wonderful reading. The story of the country boy from Owosso, Michigan, who cleaned up the white-slave ring in the big city fascinated the readers of the New York papers and even more those of the small-town dailies and weeklies. Mothers around the nation knew that now their daughters, if by some chance they ever went to New York, would be safe from a life of shame.

Up to 1937 Dewey had served only in appointive office, earlier in the federal attorney's office in New York and then as special rackets prosecutor. But in 1937 he began running for elective office. He was elected District Attorney of New York County in 1937 on the same ticket as La Guardia for mayor, and in 1938 he ran for governor, to lose to Herbert Lehman by a narrow margin. In the gubernatorial race his appeal to the voters in the rural areas began to show at the polls for the first time.

In the nation it was the reams of publicity in the small newspapers all over the country that allowed him, just a District Attorney of one county in one city, and a defeated candidate for governor, to go to the Philadelphia convention of the Republican Party in 1940 as the leading contender for the party's presidential nomination. He received 360 votes on the first ballot, but the Dewey supporters were not really firmly committed, and he was rapidly passed by Robert A. Taft and Wendell L. Willkie, the latter the eventual nominee.

But in the state Dewey, at first the white hope of the party leadership, rapidly became its master. The GOP had been plagued for years by the fact that its basic rural vote would not come to the polls in a nonpresidential year for an urban New Yorker, and the city voters, Republicans as well as Democrats, never showed any enthusiasm for an up-state "apple-knocker." Dewey seemed the answer to the party's prayer. He could get votes in both places.

His renomination for governor in 1942 was a natural one, and while his chances of getting elected did not look too good in the spring of the year, by the time he was nominated the Democrats had split, with Jim Farley in control of the old organization and with New Dealers backing a third-party ticket. Dewey's election was assured. After he was nominated, with election six weeks away, his campaign manager asked a cynical newspaper reporter what Dewey should do in the way of campaigning. "Break a leg and stay in bed for the duration," he was told.

Dewey stayed on his feet, but did little else. He made several speeches formally "opening" his campaign, and several more "closing" it, with no campaign in between. He has since been accused of never deviating from that original policy.

As Governor, however, he assumed complete control of his party. County leaders who opposed him were broken by cold, hard-bitten use of the patronage powers of the Governor's office. Legislators suffered a similar fate. He brooked no interference. In addition, he established in Albany the most elaborate public-relations set-up the capital had ever seen. Besides his own extensive secretariat, veteran newspapermen and speech-writers were hired and placed on departmental and legislative payrolls to spread the Dewey doctrine that the state was getting the best government it had ever known. Dewey was an efficient administrator and a competent Governor. In the first role he was better than Roosevelt, but he did not approach the stature of Smith and Lehman in either. Still, in his campaigns he used the characterization of "twenty years of cobwebs and dry rot" to apply to the administrations of his Democratic predecessors. He got away with it, too. His declarations that the efficiency of the state government was at an all-time peak carried weight with the public for the reason that they remained unchallenged by the Democrats, right up to campaign time, when it is always too late. A man's record can be built up or demolished in between campaigns, but once the campaign starts, the public takes anything said about him with a grain of salt.

The Democrats in the state just rolled over and played dead when Dewey assumed the Governorship. Their state committee was headed at the time by Farley, who was being ignored by the Democratic national administration. His group, having no patronage to give, remained almost dormant until he resigned as state chairman in 1944. The party's legislative leadership, which had depended for years on control of the Governor's office for its research and publicity men, and for its leadership as well, was not equipped to carry on the fight.

They let Dewey go into the 1944 presidential and 1946 gubernatorial campaigns without even challenging his claims of "tax reduction." Actually, his administration collected hundreds of millions of dollars more in taxes than any administration in history. In the controversial field of state aid for education, Dewey four times claimed and received credit for increasing the amount available, but in reality it was only subsequent increases that exceeded the total appropriated before the GOP, under Dewey's direction, began cutting the educational system.

There were countless opportunities for the Democrats to capitalize on a suspicion of Dewey's motivation in the minds of large sections of the public, but they were so disorganized that they never took advantage of them until the spring of 1948, too late to have appreciable effect. Thus, in his 1946 campaign for re-election as Governor, Dewey went before a public that passed on his record without having heard any criticism of it and was therefore convinced his performances were as good as he had described them. He won by a majority of 687,000, short of Roosevelt's 725,000 in 1930 and Lehman's 808,000 in 1934.

The Dewey battery of press agents swung into action the day after election and immediately claimed the victory to be the greatest ever scored in the state. It was, technically, the greatest majority, since the race was the first involving only two candidates in many years, owing to the fact that various minor-party nominees had been ruled off the ballot by the courts.

The victory, however, if not as great as claimed, was nevertheless an overwhelming one, and it had two principal effects, apart from continuing GOP control of the state. The first was to make Dewey's record in his first term no longer open to successful political attack, since it had been approved by the public. The second was to project him, for the third time, into the field of Republican presidential possibilities.

Dewey had won the Republican nomination in 1944—rather, it was handed to him on a platter because the party nationally felt it could not possibly defeat Franklin Roosevelt's fourth-term candidacy unless it could carry New York. And Dewey, who had won in 1942 and had been able to elect a Lieutenant Governor in a 1943 by-election, seemed to have more chance than anyone else of beating Roosevelt in his home state. The Republican diagnosis did not turn out to be correct; Dewey lost the state by more than Willkie had four years before.

Dewey had not really wanted to run in 1944, though he opened the window for his own "draft" movement. He was pretty sure it was not a good year. But he also felt that if he did not run, the nomination in 1948, probably a much

34

better time, would go to some man who had gone into uniform, rather than public office, on our entry into the war. Running in 1944 would give him a claim and the national connections for 1948, he felt, despite the precedent that a defeated candidate had never before been renominated by the Republicans.

In the years that followed his 1944 defeat, Dewey added to, rather than lost, prestige in the state. Although, while a presidential probability, he had vetoed a state FEPC law at the 1944 session of the Legislature, he generally received credit for the enactment of such a measure—the first in the nation—the following year. He won kudos also for the fact that New York State had its own rent-control law on the books during the period when national controls were temporarily lifted.

He built up the Republican party organization in New York City, and also up-state, with men with the capacity for getting out the vote, who were also loyal to him. Beyond his administrative ability, which is considerable, is his background as a good trial lawyer. This leads to insistence on being prepared for every possible contingency in the presentation of a case to the jury or an election to the public. He has many weaknesses on the personal side, most of them stemming from the unlimited power or sense of power he had in his first big job, the rackets prosecution. His word was law then in New York County, and he made it so later in New York State.

Chapter III

THE VOTERS

There is a widespread belief that the decisive factor in elections is the desire to vote against someone; that, come election day, the electorate picks up its axes and marches off to the polls determined to cut off political heads. This theory that the people always vote to negate rather than to affirm is voiced by the professional politicians and is widely accepted as gospel. It is only a half-truth. Sometimes it happens, sometimes it doesn't.

In 1920, for example, there was a definitely negative kick-the-rascals-out type of vote. The people, wearied of the strains and controls of World War I, wanted no more of the Democratic Party, which happened to be in power. In 1932, after three years of depression coinciding with a Republican administration, any Democrat would have been elected. No Republican could have done much better at the polls than hapless Herbert Hoover. And in 1946, the first election held after World War II, there was a repetition of 1920.

But in between, the trend was exactly the opposite. In 1924 and 1928 the people voted affirmatively, all over the nation, for more "prosperity." Apart from the group of Southern states that went Republican for the first time, on a religious issue, prosperity was a more important factor in 1928 than was the fear that Al Smith's election would bring the Pope to the White House.

And in 1936, 1940, and 1944 more people went to the

polls to keep Franklin Roosevelt in the Presidency, to carry on whatever he was doing at those particular times, than to vote "that man" out of there. At this writing, the 1948 candidates have not been nominated and trends are not conclusive. But in the eight key national elections preceding, the score, we can see, was at least five to three against the superstition that the political eunuch makes the best candidate, and the party that stands for the least gets the most votes. In New York State the score is even more convincing in favor of the affirmative theory, since in both the 1924 and the 1928 election the public simultaneously voted for continued Republican rule of the nation and continued Democratic rule in Albany.

In the cities of New York the voters have affirmed administrations time and time again. The people of Albany have always voted for the kind of machine government given them by the O'Connells; in Rochester they have approved the paternalism of the big-business municipal government run by Eastman Kodak and Bausch & Lomb, no matter how they have voted on state or national issues. In New York City La Guardia won re-election even when the enrollment of the voters was as high as four to one in favor of the opposing Democratic machines.

There always have been and always will be elections where the party in power is in Dutch with the voters, and then the safest course for the party out of power is to do nothing to neutralize that antipathy. The Republican congressional record preceding the 1946 elections is a classic example of such tactics.

But there probably will always be more times when popular approval will sustain a record of achievement and the outs will be able only to imitate the program of the ins and argue: "We can do it better." The over-all view of the intelligence of the voters in New York State is a good one. Where important things are concerned, their ability to

comprehend and make the right political judgments is remarkable. And New York requires no intelligence test for
its voters. All that is required of a citizen over twenty-one
years of age is that he or she be able to read simple English
and be a resident of the state for one year, the county or
city for four months, and the election district or precinct
for thirty days prior to election day.

About two decades ago, when Al Smith was reorganizing
the entire structure of the state government, the Legislature, driven by his whip, passed a series of proposed constitutional amendments to be duly submitted to the people for
final ratification at a general election. One of Al's proposed
reforms—later enacted—called for extension of the governor's term from two to four years. But the Legislature,
Republican-controlled and political-minded, in this instance
pulled a fast one. It fixed a four-year term, but scheduled
the elections for presidential election years. The Republicans had a better chance in those days of electing a governor
in the national-campaign years. The governmental effect
would have been a perpetual intertwining of state and national issues.

Smith opposed the amendment as submitted and took his
case to the people. The amendment was No. 6 of nine on
the ballot. The public defeated No. 6 and approved the
other eight. And, just to show it was not an accident, almost
exactly the same thing happened a decade later, in 1938. A
state constitutional convention held that year submitted
nine amendments, on six of which there was substantial
agreement. But proposed amendments Nos. 2, 3, and 5 ran
counter to the then prevailing New Deal voting tendencies
of the electorate. The public, by a wide margin, voted approval of amendments Nos, 1, 4, 6, 7, 8, and 9 and by equal
majorities defeated Nos. 2, 3, and 5.

In voting for major offices—governor or president—the
state's voters show no hesitancy in leaving their party, as a

glance at the vote in the last six state-wide elections will show:

YEAR	DEMOCRATIC	REPUBLICAN	ALP	LIBERAL
1936	3,018,298	2,180,670	274,924	
1938	1,971,307	2,302,505	419,979	
1940	2,834,500	3,027,478	417,418	
1942	1,501,039	2,148,546	403,626	
1944	2,478,598	2,987,647	496,505	329,235
1946	1,532,161	2,825,633	428,903	177,418

NOTE: The Liberal Party appeared on the ballot for the first time in 1944. Except for the election of 1942 the Democratic, American Labor, and Liberal parties had the same heads of the ticket, so that the Democrats carried the state, with help, in all but the 1942 and 1946 elections. Dewey in 1938 polled 24,387 additional votes on the Independent Progressive ticket, making his total 2,326,892.

While the electorate may take credit for independence and intelligent or at least understanding voting on major issues, it must accept a demerit for the little interest it shows and the lack of intelligence it uses in voting on candidates for minor offices. Many a scoundrel, nincompoop, or mediocrity has won election after election, until he has attained legislative seniority in the local board of aldermen, in the Albany Legislature, or in Congress, just because he was far enough down on the ballot line to avoid attracting attention.

If he has managed somehow to avoid indictment for larceny or arrest for wife-beating, the public at large does not recall his name and simply votes under the party emblem. The independence of thought the public uses in making its choice for the top of the ticket seems to diminish progressively as its fingers move across the voting machines toward the nominees for lesser office. For example, in Democratic New York City the Democratic majorities, though not the total vote cast, increase in each assembly district the

39

farther one gets away from the head of the ticket, so that many an anonymous assemblyman has won by a greater margin than Roosevelt, the greatest vote-getter his party ever had. And in up-state Republican territory a candidate on the GOP ticket for the same office would always win by more votes than Tom Dewey.

What happens is that in territory known to be "safe" for one party or another, the opposition and the independents do not bother voting for offices contained in that political unit, but do vote for state-wide offices, for which, they figure, they have a chance of affecting the actual result. Also, the independents do not vote for minor offices when they do not know the candidates, while the party regulars just vote the straight ticket, all the way down the line. And some who do bolt their party at the top of the ticket often salve their conscience by voting "regular" the rest of the way.

There are exceptions. In 1940 a number of Democratic legislators from Brooklyn were at odds with their party's state and national policies. They didn't like Roosevelt, Lehman, or their own legislative leadership and they all but campaigned openly for Willkie. They indicated they thought their loyal followers should vote Republican at the top of the ticket. Many did, and too many of these forgot to return to the Democratic column on the ballot. Willkie carried the districts and so did the Republican nominees for the Legislature. The results, known afterward in Albany as the "bloodless purge," proved something politicians have always contended: that it is a dangerous thing to start teaching party regulars how to cut a ticket. They may cut a throat.

Sometimes a man who has run for years for secondary office, but never at the head of a ticket, gets such large majorities that he and his friends really become convinced that he is an attractive vote-getter in his own right, that he can win any office.

Jim Mead of Buffalo was one of these. A tall, well-built handshaker, he won fourteen straight elections to the state Assembly and to the House of Representatives, to become one of the few Northerners to have substantial congressional seniority. Then he was elected twice to the United States Senate by big majorities in years when the public's interest was on the Governorship or on the Presidency. To his friends he looked unbeatable and they produced figures that seemed to prove it, at least to their own satisfaction. But he ran for governor, as the head of the ticket, in a year when it was tough for his party, against an opponent who was well known, and the public retired Mead from politics with gusto.

In Brooklyn—always safe Democratic territory—John N. Harman, an amiable newspaper publisher and amateur politician, consistently led the ticket in majorities while running for such offices as county clerk and county register. He tried to run for city comptroller, the second most important post in the city government, and though he was the organization designee, he never even got past the primary election. Nor did he carry Brooklyn in that preliminary test within his own party.

In New York State as a whole there is a tendency to oversimplify the normal voting habits of the state electorate by explaining that "rural" up-state, the fifty-seven counties outside the big city limits of New York, votes Republican and that New York City votes Democratic.

This ignores the tendency of the boroughs of Queens and Richmond, inside the city, to vote against the New Deal in elections when that was an issue, and it overlooks completely the sentiment of the industrial belt that runs across the middle of the state—from Troy through Albany, Utica,

Syracuse and Rochester to Buffalo. Albany and Utica are Democratic strongholds, Syracuse and Rochester have Republican machines that are consistently supported by the voters, Troy and Buffalo swing first one way and then the other.

The population in these cities more closely parallels that of New York City than it does that of the countryside surrounding them, and the resemblance shows up in the vote. If there is going to be a Democratic landslide in New York City, the Democrats should win, or make a close race of it, in all the cities along the main line of the New York Central's water-level route. If the Democratic ticket is destined to bring nothing but an apathetic response in New York City, then the cousins in the up-state cities go into hiding and the wave rolls state-wide in the other direction, drowning any Democratic candidate rash enough to be in the political swim that year. Thus is created an extremely wide swing of the political pendulum, capable of giving the Democrats a million majority one year and the Republicans nearly as big a margin only a few years later.

The proportion of truly rural residents to the whole population of the state has declined for many years, and whereas elections once could be won on the dairy farms of the north country and the fruit orchards of mid-state, now they are settled in the villages and small cities as well as in the large urban centers.

The 1940 federal census listed 11,165,000 residents as "urban" and only 2,313,000 as "rural," and everything indicates that the shifting of population brought on by the war and the war-production effort drew even more away from the farms.

The division of the voters into the two major parties goes far back into American history. It was the city man against the farmer a hundred years ago, the immigrant against the third-generation American, the Irish against the Britishers who populated up-state New York. In more modern times the differences showed up principally in the willingness of the city dweller to approve governmental experiments, while the rural folk, attached to the never changing land, remained conservative. The cities of the state voted for the Roosevelt New Deal as they never had voted for anything else. In the country areas, it enjoyed only a temporary popularity, pretty well exhausted by the end of 1936. In New York, as elsewhere in the nation, the dislike of the farmer for city ways has the effect, the Solid South excepted, of putting the farmers in an opposite political party.

Religious beliefs, racial backgrounds, and the influence of events abroad on our thinking have always played a part in American elections despite our desire to look the other way when specific examples are mentioned. We have had the Know-Nothing movement and the Klan. In 1916 the Germans voted for Wilson because he "kept us out of war" with their homeland. In 1919 Tammany Hall, Irish stronghold, failed to elect local candidates because Wilson, the Democratic President, was not supporting the cause of Irish freedom, a very close parallel to the position in which the Democrats found themselves on the Jewish homeland question early in 1948.

No major party has ever dared nominate a Jew for the Presidency and only once has a Catholic been named. In the last decade the effect of racial and religious stress and strain and of events abroad has been more and more noticeable in New York, the original melting-pot. The late Jimmy Walker used to start off a speech in which he had nothing particular to say with the statement that New York City had more Irish than Dublin, more Jews than Jerusalem, more Italians than Rome, more Greeks than Athens, and so on. His comparisons were limited only by his geographical recollections on that particular evening. Jimmy used his figures, most of them accurate, to prove what a great city he ran and how the members of so many different races could live side by side without political conflict.

He was only partly right. Given a particular set of circumstances, the voters may follow racial or religious lines, to the exclusion of other considerations, in some particular election. The Jews never voted as a unit for any member of their race until Herbert Lehman came along. He was probably the best representative of the Hebrews ever to run for high administrative office and they voted for him en masse in all but one of his campaigns. Fiorello H. La Guardia, of mixed Italian and Jewish stock, got many Jewish votes, but they were cast for the man and his political creed.

The Jews did not flock to the polls to vote for Albert Ottinger, or for Jonah J. Goldstein, the badly beaten candidate for mayor of New York City in 1945. But they did vote almost as a unit for Franklin D. Roosevelt in 1940 and 1944 because he represented to them the world leadership of the fight against Hitlerism and they viewed him also as a bulwark against anti-Semitism in the United States. The Jews split on Lehman, to a very minor extent, when he ran for United States senator in 1946 because his record on the Palestine question was not then pleasing to the most ardent Zionists.

In the case of the Irish, they became Democrats and joined Tammany Hall in New York City when they first came here in great numbers as a result of the potato famine in the old country. Those who later moved up-state kept their Democratic affiliations. It was their party, and politics was their pastime, if not their living. Look over the names of the leaders of the party organizations, Tammany and its city and up-state allies, and you find no names but those of the Murphys and the Kellys, the Flynns and Crokers, McCooeys, McCarrens, and McKanes. The Irish vote was nearly always so "safe" that Charles Francis Murphy of

Tammany Hall was constantly on the lookout for some good Protestant to run for public office, to pick up some additional support. The Irish were his, regardless. The O'Connell organization in Albany has always operated on the same theory, selecting its mayors from the families of the original Dutch settlers, all Protestants.

From time immemorial, politicians have tried to "balance" a ticket, by picking a list of candidates from different sections of the state, and also making sure that the predominant racial groups were represented, not so much because of their extra votes as to prevent the opposition from picturing the group not represented as being discriminated against. A companion theory usually adhered to is that a man who has left the church he was born into for another should not be nominated. Many a religious apostate well qualified for high office has been ruled out by the reasoning that the adherents of the denomination he left will be bitter about it, while he will attract no additional support among those of his new faith. James F. Byrnes was eliminated from the vice-presidential nomination by Roosevelt in 1944 on those grounds. In New York the issue was raised publicly against Charles Poletti in 1938 when he was a candidate for lieutenant governor, but Poletti was able to prove his choice had been made for him at the tender age of four, and he was forgiven, at least sufficiently for him to win an election. A boom for James Forrestal for governor in 1946 was dropped when it became known he was no longer a communicant in the Catholic Church. Peculiarly, the issue is never raised in connection with appointment, rather than election, to office.

Because of its large number of devout communicants, the Catholic Church has always been a force to be considered in state politics. And because the church is in general conservative in its leanings and its teachings, there was the beginning, as early as 1936, of an Irish-Catholic defection from the Democratic Party in the state because of charges that the New Deal was radical.

This increased in importance as the Democrats continued their alliance with the American Labor Party and as they tied up with the Political Action Committee of the CIO in 1944. The Pope meanwhile had assumed world leadership in the fight against Communism, the Catholic Church locally was preaching the evils of the Soviet system, and many Irish felt there was at least a glimmer of truth in the charges that the Communists, by infiltration into the ALP and the PAC, were allied with the Democrats. Their religion began to weaken their inherited party ties.

This reached a high level in 1946. Ranking political leaders of both major parties felt that year that the church was out to strike a definite blow at Communism; they received what they took to be authorized notice that the political effect would be to hit at the alliance between the Democrats and the left-wingers by a vote against their candidates. Officially the church made no moves, but the vote on election day indicated that Catholics had followed the line the party leaders had been told about. In the state election the protest involved voting for a Republican ticket composed entirely of Protestants against a Democratic ticket headed by an Irish Catholic. The turn the Truman administration took so sharply to the political right following the election can be attributed at least in part to a desire to recapture the Catholic vote in New York City and in other big centers of Catholicism in the nation.

Another of the great racial groups to be reckoned with in New York elections is the Italians. They have not been permanently anchored in either party and have shown a greater tendency toward clannishness in their voting than either the Irish or the Jews. The Italian candidate for public office has nearly always been able to count on support from his countrymen even if they sometimes did not approve his policies. The two major parties, made aware of this by the successes of Poletti and La Guardia, have tried in recent years to make sure of having an Italian candidate on their state ticket. The Italians in New York were Republicans in their voting tendencies up to the Roosevelt era, when they switched to the Democratic side.

In dealing with the impact of racial remembrances on elections it should be remembered that it isn't only recent immigrants and their offspring who are affected. In the presidential election of 1944 Roosevelt had the potential support of a large number of voters of English, Welsh, and Scotch ancestry who wanted him to carry on as commander-in-chief and to win the war that would preserve old England. This was so not only in New York but in New Jersey, Connecticut, and Massachusetts. These voters were too conservative politically, however, to take Henry Wallace too. Most of them were Republicans. Roosevelt, with an eye to the key electoral votes of the four states, ditched Wallace as the vice-presidential nominee and named Truman. He figured that the votes for Wallace had nowhere else to go, anyway.

That is what Edward J. Flynn in his book *You're the Boss* meant when, talking of the selection of Truman, he said it had been made on the grounds that it would hurt the Roosevelt candidacy the least.

There was still another ethnological factor working in favor of Roosevelt in both the 1940 and the 1944 elections. The Greeks, the Poles, the Serbs, and the Czechs wanted to ensure the defeat of Hitler and Hitlerism, and this, they felt, would be best accomplished by re-electing Roosevelt, the interventionist of 1940 and the wartime leader of 1944.

But by 1946 this policy had gone into reverse. The war was over, Roosevelt was dead, the peace had not been won. It was perfectly evident to those making political canvasses in the spring of that year that things were going to be rough on the party in power unless the situation improved by early fall. Not only were the Irish Catholics concerned about the spread of Communism. The Poles did not like the division of Poland, the Italians were unhappy about the fate of Italy, there were starvation and civil war in Greece and disorder in Palestine, and the Iron Curtain had descended on the Balkans. In the tumult of the autumn campaign the visible issues were the shortages of goods and services, the lack of meat and housing. But there was also good reason to believe that the minds of many voters were made up in the spring on the basis of racial and religious factors that had nothing to do with the price of pork chops. High prices contributed to a Democratic defeat already in the making.

The Negro vote, of increasing importance as the percentage of the black or brown population grows and achieves literacy through schooling once out of its reach, has fluctuated between the major parties in recent elections. It was Republican, following pretty blindly the party of Lincoln, until the Roosevelt era. The mass of the Harlem Negroes believed in Roosevelt and even more particularly in Mrs. Roosevelt. After Roosevelt died, Dewey courted the Negroes with appointments to high office, and this, coupled with the reascendance to power of the Southern Democrats in Washington, was swinging the Negroes back to the GOP at the end of 1947.

The proportional-representation method of electing City Council members in New York City for the decade between 1937 and 1947 played a part in fanning racial feeling at the polls. This method had the advantage of freeing candidates for the council from the necessity of being nominated in a machine-dominated primary election, but to those who followed the day-to-day transfer of votes in its cumbersome system of multiple counts the processes revealed were sometimes shocking.

Joe Murphy, an ardent exponent of the principles of the Christian Front, might be eliminated from the race on the fourth transfer of choices, and of his ten thousand assorted votes probably as many as eight thousand would go to Joe McShane, also an Irishman, but a Communist or at least a fellow traveler. Simon Schwartz, old-time Socialist, would lose out and most of his votes would go to Shapiro, a labor-baiting dress-manufacturer. Salvatore would get the votes of Santini. There would be no rhyme nor reason for these transfers except that furnished by a racial similarity of names, coupled with alphabetical proximity on the paper ballot. The only candidates who did not gain because of race were the Negroes. Their names showed no blacker on the ballots than those of their white competitors.

This chapter has thus far stressed the influence of race and creed on voting. It would not do to overstress that influence. In recent years it assumed unusual proportions, possibly temporary, because of the general tension in the world, because all peoples seemed deprived of the security they desired so much. But in the long run no party is assured of continued success by appealing to the voters on racial lines alone. The voters get tired of it. They mark a candidate down as a professional Irishman, Jew, Italian, or Negro, as the case may be. Sometimes appeals made strictly on racial issues backfire immediately. One can remember Joe Mc-Williams, who started running for Congress in German Yorkville on a race-hate program resembling Hitler's in the days immediately preceding our entrance into World War II. McWilliams entered the Republican primary, and overnight the entire strength of the Republican Party in New York County was thrown in against him. The Republican county chairman was farsighted enough to know that the party could not afford, either in the county or in the state at large, to welcome as one of its own a man who espoused Hitler's anti-Semitic program as well as other Hitlerian concepts.

McWilliams was defeated and he disappeared from the local political scene. Had he and his district been left alone, he conceivably could have been nominated. But over a period of years the public votes as employees and employers, as members of the American Legion, as civil-service workers, as housewives and insurance brokers, besides voting as Jews, Catholics, Protestants, or Mohammedans. There is the labor vote, the highbrow vote, the farm vote and the business vote, the regular Democratic, Republican, Labor, Liberal, and Communist party vote. Heaven help the forecaster who attempts to divide the electorate along one set of lines and forgets the others! An Irish war veteran, enrolled as a Democrat, who is also a dues-paying member of a labor union, is likely to be counted on the basis of each affiliation —in this case four times. Just for the record, lest I be accused of overlooking the obvious, I will note that the most important factor controlling the vote, in New York or any place else, is the economic factor. "People vote their pocketbooks" is an old saying, the truth of which was borne out just recently by the success of the 1946 Republican slogan "Had Enough? Vote Republican," at a time when prices were rising and goods shortages were plaguing merchant and housewife alike. It was far and away the most important element in the 1932 Hoover debacle.

Sometimes election claims of organized group support are amusing. There was a candidate for mayor of New York who did not particularly deserve election and whose campaign publicity men, even, were hard put to it to think up anything printable to say about him. But they tried hard, and the newspapers each day received statements of endorsement of the great man attributed to leaders of various racial and economic groups. They pledged the votes of half a million Poles, three hundred thousand Greeks, a million Italians. The Jews, the Irish, the Ethiopians were for him, as were the police and firemen and all city employees, 125,-000 strong, to say nothing of half a million dues-paying members of organized labor. By election day the support claimed for him totaled 6,000,000 votes, nearly the total population of the city at that time. Actually 2,000,000 votes were cast for all candidates, and he received 580,000.

At least two candidates for state-wide office have been given major-party nominations in recent years because they were supposed to have the support of all the state employees, then about 70,000 strong. To debunk this one can use a rough rule of thumb. About 40,000 already belonged to the same party as these nominees and would have voted for them in the absence of some reason to change. Probably 20,000 more were rock-ribbed members of the opposition, and only the remaining 10,000 were left to be influenced by the individualities of the candidates and other calculable factors such as the economic conditions of the state and nation.

It might be added that neither candidate won and neither showed any special vote-getting strength. The same breakdown of claimed support must be applied to the American Legion vote, the Jewish vote, the Catholic vote, or any other, barring the special circumstances described before.

There is a strong resemblance between an election and a show on Broadway. If a good, exciting one is in the making, the people come out in droves and S. R. O. signs are hung in the registration and election booths. Let it be a desultory, decided-in-advance contest between two men of no particular appeal and the box-office draw is about equal to that of *The Ladder*, the play to which, one may remember, they couldn't give away tickets.

To show the difference in appeal, take the presidential

contests of 1940 and 1944. They were good close races, though not so close as they seemed to the public, and the issues were burning. So 6,301,596 voted in the state in 1940, and four years later 6,316,750 voted, despite the loss of many potential soldier ballots owing to a clumsy soldier-vote law. But in between, in 1942, the people were invited to a three-cornered gubernatorial race with the result determined in advance in favor of Dewey by reason of a Democratic party split. Only 4,177,075 came to the polls, the smallest number in recent political history. Dewey's first appearance, in 1938, four years earlier, drew a larger gate by 650,000.

Despite the fluctuation from election to election, determined by the office at stake and the issues in any given year, the trend of the vote has been steadily upward, and not only because of the increase in the actual population. It is hard to believe now that the presidential election of 1920 attracted only 2,898,513 voters in the state, as against the 6,301,596 of twenty years later. The first represented 27.9 per cent of the total population of the state, the latter 46.7 per cent.

There are a number of reasons for the increase. First, the percentage of aliens in the population, ineligible to vote, has dropped off steadily owing to naturalization of those already here and the cutting off of the flow of new immigrants in the early twenties. Secondly, women, who began voting in national elections in 1920, have taken increasing advantage of their new right. In any number of recent elections the enrollment figures, a rough but adequate guide, indicate that as many women as men have voted. Thirdly, the age level of the population has increased; people live longer and the number alive over the age of twenty-one is greater than ever before.

A fourth factor, one probably accountable for more new votes than any one of the others, is the increased political consciousness of the people. During the Roosevelt era they began to see more and more the tie-up between politics and the pocketbook, between government and groceries. They started voting, either for or against Roosevelt, and it turned into a habit.

Chapter IV

WHAT MAKES A PARTY

The night of October 6, 1932 produced in New York City a most remarkable political meeting. The 32,075 members of the Democratic county committees of the five counties in the Greater City had been summoned by postcard to Madison Square Garden, and 20,000 showed up. The purpose of the meeting, required by law to be stated in advance, was to "nominate" a candidate for mayor to succeed dapper Jimmy Walker, who had resigned just in time to forestall his removal by Governor Franklin D. Roosevelt. Election of whoever was nominated was certain, since the eyes of the voters were on national affairs that year and Tammany's scandals could be dealt with the following year, when a full four-year mayoralty tenure would be at stake.

The Garden, biggest hall in the city, wasn't big enough to hold all the committeemen entitled to attend. It barely held those who showed up. The meeting was started by a calling of the roll, as required by law. A succession of leather-lunged secretaries blaahed out names that were completely indistinguishable, for a period that seemed interminable. Actually the roll-call lasted two and a half hours, and observers could only assume that all the names had been read.

It didn't matter, since not a soul was sure enough that his name was being called to dare an answer. But a quorum was declared present, the meeting was under way, and the rest was much easier and quicker. A recognized lieutenant

of the boss of Tammany Hall presented the name of John
P. O'Brien, an obscure surrogate, as the party's candidate
for mayor, and his was the only name presented. O'Brien
was then declared nominated by acclamation. The few
thousands who had remained to the dismal end sauntered
out of the hall, to home and bed, or possibly a near-by
speakeasy.

Except for its huge size, the meeting afforded a perfect
example of the state's established political machinery at
work. The unwieldy, too big county committee could not
function as the house of delegates it was supposed to be.
Nor did it have any real desire to do so. The committee was
there, and those who attended knew so in advance, merely
to ratify a candidate previously hand-picked by the bosses.
What happened that night on a city-wide basis occurs all
the time on a county-wide or district basis in all the established political parties.

New York has a direct primary system and election law
which is tied in very closely with the structure of the political parties. The law legalizes the parties and regulates their
acts, much more so than in most states. The election law
itself is hundreds of pages in length, designed to cover all
contingencies. Most of it was written to replace the old party
caucus system, which placed boss rule beyond any challenge.

The system in effect in the state now does not prevent
boss rule, but it does leave a loophole, through the direct
primary system, for a revolt against the machine by a really
aroused electorate. This happens only once or twice in a
generation.

The conclave in Madison Square Garden was called because Walker had resigned too late in the political year for
a primary election to be held. The election law—and in
New York State it is in general a good law—specifies in true
democratic fashion that if a vacancy occurs in any political
office for which nominations would normally be made at a

primary, the county committee of the appropriate unit, the area in which the candidate must run, shall name the party's nominee. In this case the appropriate political unit was the city at large, with 3,700 election districts at that time.

All that the committee members did at the Garden was what they normally do: rubber-stamp decisions already made by the bosses, local, county, or municipal. In this case they actually had to meet, because a binding legal nomination was being made. In most cases, on other items, they delegate their powers in advance—give them away within a week after their own election.

This is how the system works. The power to control a political party in New York State is vested in its enrolled voters. Operating under the election law, with ballots paid for out of the public treasury, they choose county and state committees of their party at primary elections and, whether they realize it or not, delegate to these men and women control of the party. These county and state committee members are the "organization," the active party workers, the "ward-heelers" if you will. Right after they are elected they pass their powers on in turn by electing executive committee members, who also pass them on to the leader or chairman. He is the boss, and he is fortified in his position by the fact that the party rules, once adopted at the county or state committee meeting, held every two years, have the force of law unless they conflict with the actual written election law.

These rules vary, even within the parties. One unusually democratic rule, in force in Brooklyn, makes the man who is elected state committeeman by the party voters also the ward or district boss. He is thus chosen directly by the voters, whereas in most other counties the local leader is chosen by the county committee members and his name never appears on the primary ballot. In New York County, Tammany Hall, by its own rules, has kept the county committee so large—it furnished 19,000 of the 32,000 mentioned above—that it can never function effectively on a county-wide basis.

A word about the election law. Though passed by the Legislature, it is actually written by the legal counsel of the two major political parties and designed by them to make smoother the functioning of their machinery within the principles of a primary system and free elections that the public has shown it wants. While the two old established parties have the legal cards stacked slightly in their favor, since they got into the game first, there is no broad legal discrimination against the two newer parties, or even against minor political groups. It is an anomaly that while the Legislature has passed several laws aimed at preventing Communists from holding civil-service or exempt appointive posts, it has not attempted, through 1948, to prevent their possible election to office.

The four established parties in the state, recognized as legal under the election law, are, in order of the size of the vote they have polled in recent years, the Republican, Democratic, American Labor, and Liberal parties. The fact that they are "legal" does not mean that others, including the Communists, are illegal and have to go underground. It merely means that the four principal groups polled at least 50,000 votes for governor in the most recent gubernatorial election and that they are therefore entitled to hold primary elections at public expense, enroll members, make party rules that are legally binding, and pick delegates, under recognized legal auspices, to their own county, state, and national conventions.

Political groups in existence at this writing that have not attained or retained legal status include the Communist, Socialist, Workers', and Industrial Government parties. They are called political groups and get on the ballot only by obtaining signatures to nominating petitions. Their principal legal right is the protection of their names, which may not be used by candidates without the permission of their central committees. Since all the independent groups in the state put together rarely poll more than two per cent of the total vote, the concern must be with the established legal political parties, with their vast memberships.

Nearly all in New York State who take the trouble to vote also take the trouble to "join" their political party. Why they do it is not clear, since the vast majority never interest themselves in party affairs after joining and have little conception of the right of control the party primary gives them. Maybe they join just because the membership is free. Of course, in an area where one party is dominant, there is a tendency to join in order to ensure at least a friendly reception if there should be occasion to apply to a party leader for a favor.

Occasionally some unusually determined voter turns up, like the New York City Democrat who moved to Republican Dutchess County. He enrolled there as a Republican, hoping some day for the opportunity to vote against Hamilton Fish in the congressional primary. He waited five years before he got his chance.

The process of joining a party is remarkably simple. Each year when the voters trek to the polls in October to register for the November election—an annual event everywhere except in the strictly rural regions—they are handed, in the registration booths, slips of paper entitling them to check themselves off as members of the four parties. The number who do so is startlingly high. In New York City it runs year after year as much as ninety-five per cent of the total who register. In the sixty-two cities of the state, New York City included, all but 360,000 enrolled out of 4,866,000 who registered in 1940. There was about the same number of abstentions in 1942, but the complicating factor of the soldier ballot prevented as high a percentage of enrollment in 1944. In 1946 it was back to normal, with 3,578,000 enrolling out of 3,893,000 who registered in the cities.

Figures for the state as a whole cannot be used as an accurate guide, since in the country areas registration and enrollment are permanent, not annual, and in one rural county the registry books may have been cleared of deadwood the year before, and in another not for two decades. By enrolling in a party the voters acquire the right to vote in the primary of that party, and no other, the following year. This lapse of time—registration one year with enrollment, and primary privileges delayed to the next—makes the New York primary a "closed primary" as compared with that in Wisconsin, called "open" because there any voter can vote in the primary of any party, any year, after the issues have arisen. At the primary, as noted, the voters pick their party nominees for public office, and their party officers as well.

Their choice lies in three separate groups. The first of these consists of the candidates for public office. In New York State the party voters, or as many of them as are willing to take the trouble, pick at the primary election all candidates for Congress and the state Legislature, for lower court judgeships, for mayor and local officers generally. Anyone who can get the necessary number of signatures on a petition—and the number varies depending on the area to be represented—and who is a member of the party, a recently added requirement, is entitled to have his name on the primary ballot. If he gets the highest number of votes, he becomes the party nominee. Often this assures in advance his election to the office he is seeking, but just as often he is doomed to run only for the exercise, depending on the status of his party in the region. Which it is going to be cannot always be foretold. A Republican nomination for Congress was open one year in a heavily Democratic district in Manhattan. The party leaders put in a designee who was a dummy, intending to withdraw him as soon as they found a more suitable candidate. But no one else would run, with defeat appearing so certain, and the dummy made the race. However, the Democrats became engaged in an intra-party cat-and-dog fight and split wide open, with the result that the Republican won the election, the first his party had ever achieved in that locality. Political annals contain many similar cases of nonentities achieving distinction through default.

The second group of choices involved in a primary election concerns the election of delegates. This was not in the direct primary law as originally written for New York State, but was a modification made later to take many important nominations out of the hands of the voters. It does just that. Instead of voting directly for candidates for the nomination for governor, for United States senator, or for other state offices, the enrolled voters choose delegates to a state convention, which does the picking. In the case of district judges, they vote for delegates to a judicial district convention. In that of president and vice president of the United States they vote at a special spring primary for delegates to a national convention. The entire process of electing delegates to any one of these conventions is farcical, and apparently deliberately so, since the law does not permit placing the names of any of the prospective candidates on the ballot—only the names of the delegates—and no legally binding pledge can be made by a delegate to carry out the people's choice for judge, governor, or president. Instead, the delegates are just a list of names who will vote in the convention as they are told by the bosses, who put their names on the primary ballot in the first place.

The futility of running delegates in opposition to the organization slate was demonstrated in New York in 1936 when friends of the late William E. Borah entered slates of delegates in the Republican presidential primary in several districts in Manhattan. They were pledged to Borah orally, and the organization candidates were pledged to nobody at all, not even to Alf M. Landon, who later became the party's nominee. But the Borah ticket got fewer votes in the GOP primary than its expense statement showed it had paid for in the way of free dinners for party workers. In the winter of 1947–8, Harold E. Stassen carefully weighed the possibility of entering a slate of delegates against the Dewey organization, but decided against it, even though he was an avowed candidate and Dewey was not at that time. There is an old rule in politics that "you can't beat somebody with nobody," but it doesn't apply to an election of delegates in a primary.

In the third group of choices exercised by the voters in a primary, they actually elect their legal party organizations. They choose the members of the county committee, from two to twenty members for each election district, and they choose the members of the state committee, two from each assembly district in the major parties, and five from each in the ALP and the Liberal Party. The whole legal power of the party is vested in these two committees and, theoretically at least, no overturn in party leadership in a district, a county, or the entire state can be accomplished without the consent of the majority of the committee members.

In practice, while there are frequent changes in party leadership, only once in a generation is one brought about by a primary battle for committeemen fought on a large scale. More often a change comes either because the party has suffered a disastrous defeat in the preceding election, and new leadership, even if only for window-dressing, seems desirable, or because the party has elected to office some candidate who by use of his patronage power in the county, city, or state wants and is able to swing the party leadership into different hands. The district leaders and their county committee members flop over to his side.

The voters' voice in party affairs would be much greater if more of them voted in the primary elections, but only a small percentage does. In 1943 the American Labor Party had an enrollment of roughly 180,000 in New York City, a lower percentage of its actual vote than any other party by far. But the fact that its enrollment was so low in comparison with its vote was at the same time an indication that the people enrolled were closely tied to their party. In the primary election that year, which settled party control and in which the entire state was interested, 80,000 votes were cast, or 44 per cent of the enrollment. This, instead of being a low figure, is almost a record high. As few as 10 per cent of the enrolled voters participate in the normal primary, and in the major parties the number goes as high as 25 per cent only when there is some really interesting contest involving principles and personalities.

The apathy of the enrolled voter suits the machines. On primary day they round up votes among the electorate at large only in self-defense—that is, if the party machine in the area is threatened by an insurgent. Otherwise many a voter knows of primary day only because he finds the bars and liquor stores closed between three and ten p.m., when the polls are open.

The direct primary law was set up in New York State under pressure from reformers, led by Charles Evans Hughes. The professional politicians were leery of it from the start. As the years went on, however, they found their fears were groundless in the main, and they also found more and more ways to circumvent the law's intention, which is to permit the enrolled voters to challenge the decisions of the boss or even to change the boss. Tammany's principal method of beating the primary system was to increase the size of its county committee so that in any district an insurgent slate would have to muster sometimes hundreds of committee candidates to oppose those designated by the boss, and then the insurgent slate would be subjected to intense pressure to force withdrawals. Those who didn't withdraw were likely to be thrown off the slate by "invalidation" of designating petitions. And designating petitions are easy to challenge.

As noted earlier, in order for a name to appear on a primary ballot, petitions have to be circulated and signed, the law specifying the number of signatures required.

But the law also specifies in detail how petitions shall be prepared; it requires a sworn witness to each signature, the home election district of each signer, and in general much more detail than seems necessary. Added requirements have been written into the law almost yearly, at the request of the entrenched party organizations. Still others are added by the interpretations of the boards of election, under bipartisan control, and by the courts. The intention is to make petitions by independents more easily subject to challenge and invalidation, and the boards of election, invariably representative of the ruling faction in the organization, do not shirk their duties. Let one color of ink be used in one place and a different color in another, and out goes the petition and the candidate. Let the notary who witnessed the signatures use the wrong date of expiration of his own commission, and poof goes the primary fight.

The stories of how boards of election operate to preserve the *status quo* in a party are legion. One that comes to mind is that of the perfect set of designating petitions filed one time with the New York City board by an independent candidate. The most careful study showed not a single thing wrong with them, not a technicality that had not been met. But something had to be done. So the board went into a huddle and threw out the petitions on the ground that they must be fraudulent even though they did not appear so, because it was impossible to prepare legitimately so perfect a set.

Still another is the tale of the well-known counsel to one of the major party organizations who stood smoking his cigar during a luncheon recess of hearings on petitions. A contestant whom he did not know asked:

"Were my petitions thrown out?"

"What are you, organization or insurgent?" the counsel asked.

"Insurgent."

"You're out," said the counsel.

Of course many petitions are fraudulent, at least in part. There is no way an honest candidate, with legitimate support, can prevent some made-up names and nonexistent signers from appearing on his petitions, because there always will be some signature-collectors who on a rainy afternoon will decide to do the job in a neighborhood saloon. Even when the Republican and Democratic party organizations collected 140,000 names on a petition for the repeal of proportional representation in 1947—and they possess the ultimate in petition-signing machinery—a number of errors and frauds were pointed out by the opposition.

In borderline cases coming before the boards of election, though the bipartisan membership may deadlock occasionally in a conflict involving one major party against the other, they are usually unanimous in protecting the existing organization of either party against threatened infiltration, invasion, or overthrow.

The decisions of the boards are reviewable by the courts, and in flagrant cases of abuse of power the boards are overruled. It is possible, however, for a case to be delayed so that the decision is of little use to the appellant. The state law gives election cases clear precedence on court calendars, and even the Court of Appeals convenes in special session

64

when the need arises. But no decision handed down two days before the primary or the election itself can restore the morale of an insurgent movement that for weeks has faced the possibility that its candidates' names would not be on the ballot.

Most of the "invalidation" skullduggery involves contests for district leaderships between Joe Tweedledee and Moe Tweedledum, Moe and his followers consisting of a disgruntled group of district captains who think that Joe either has been hogging the patronage or else has not been getting enough for the district because he isn't sufficiently enterprising. So the public seldom rises in its wrath; and the boards of election have the judgment not to play too rough where the public interest is really involved.

The election law in New York State is written with the intention of holding down the number of political groups that can operate on a state-wide basis. The theory, which is sound enough, is that there should be some indication of a state-wide demand for a candidate running for state office before his name should be allowed to clutter up the ballot.

So in order to run a state-wide ticket in behalf of a group that is not a legal party, twelve thousand signatures must be obtained. That part is easy, but there is an additional requirement that at least fifty of the signatures be obtained in each of the sixty-two counties of the state. And it is nearly four hundred miles from New York City to the Canadian border, and more than three hundred from Albany to Buffalo. Canvassers must cover a lot of territory. Another difficulty is that there are at least two counties in rural up-state New York where the population and vote are so small and the Republican control so complete that the GOP organization could prevent an outside group from getting fifty legal signatures in the county. Failure to get the names in a single county would keep the party off the ballot. This step, however, while often considered, has not been taken in recent years, because the independent groups are much more likely to draw votes from the Democrats than from the Republicans and it therefore does not suit the GOP's purposes to keep them off the voting machines.

It is worth noting that despite all the ideological objection to Communism and the American Communist Party that exists within the Republican Party, the Republicans could have chosen (but did not) to keep the Communists off the ballot in New York State at any time in the past decade. It would have taken some concentrated effort, but it could have been done, and it would have been legal.

It takes jobs and patronage to run a major political party, and it takes cash contributions, too. These contributions are made, for one reason or another, year in and year out by party members who can spare the cash. Some want political recognition, some want favors in the offing, some give because they have received favors in the past and do not want to seem ungracious now.

Under various laws all contributions to political parties are reported officially, either in Washington or in state capitals like Albany, and the public is supposed thereby to have information about who is supporting whom, politically, to the extent of paying the bills. That is purely theoretical. The system was inexact enough before the passage by Congress of the Hatch Act, which was supposed to legislate political morality by putting a ceiling on campaign contributions and expenditures. Now it is worse. Before the Hatch Act was enacted, the national committee of a party collected as much as it could, spent as much as it needed, and reported most of the items on both sides of its books. State committees took care of expenses within the particular state, and county committees handled purely local costs.

But the Hatch Act put a limit on the amount a national committee could collect or spend, so now the national committees of both major parties work up to that limit. Once they reach it, they shunt all additional contributions before they are formally made, and all expenditures before they are billed, to various state committees, which are not subject to congressional control. Different pockets are used for the same old purpose.

The Republicans worked out this evasion in the 1940 campaign, when the ink of the limiting legislation had barely dried on the statute books. The Democrats that year further gummed up political bookkeeping for years to come by making loans between state committees and the national committee which no one has yet been able to figure how to pay off without violating some law.

So when you see in your newspaper an account of expenditures made by the Republican National Committee or the Democratic National Committee, in the 1948 or other future campaigns, just skip over the details. They mean nothing, reflect nothing more than some individual system of evading the Hatch Act, which should never have been adopted.

If the national committee of any party should want to spend $20,000,000 on winning a presidential election and could raise the money to do so, it should be allowed to spend it, and the public should know who gave the money. It probably could figure out for itself why. There would undoubtedly be a reaction against "buying" an election which would cancel out all or part of the votes obtained by any extraordinary expenditure. Now a party is barred from spending more than $3,000,000, so that is all the public ever knows about. The rest is poured out through state committees and independent groups, and no one but the party treasurer knows how much went for any one purpose.

Another section of the Hatch Act, the original reason for the passage of the measure, bars political activity by anyone receiving federal funds or holding federal office. It has its background in the Barkley-Chandler primary fight a decade ago in Kentucky, when Barkley used the WPA and Chandler an equally powerful state machine to fight for the Democratic nomination for the United States Senate.

As a result of it postmasters and other federal employees, like collectors of internal revenue, marshals, and so on, are barred from political activity, but again only in theory. Any federal office-holder who was also a county boss and was worth his salt in the latter role just resigned the official chairmanship, put a trusted stooge in his place, and continued running party affairs from his comfortable office in the Federal Building.

There are similar situations in the state offices. In 1946, for example, Alger B. Chapman, chairman of the New York State Tax Commission, resigned that job in midsummer to run Dewey's campaign for re-election as governor. The State Tax Commission collects taxes from individuals and corporations and is in a position to make rulings favorable or unfavorable to various people, so obviously it would not do for Mr. Chapman to continue in that job and run a political campaign. As soon as Mr. Dewey was re-elected, however, Chapman was reappointed to his old post, again in charge of collecting taxes. Some might consider his original resignation a subterfuge.

The Chapman case was not an isolated one, nor is the system recent in developing. As long as one can remember, state and city employees who might be of value to their parties in a campaign have taken "leaves of absence" or "vacations" during campaign time to work for their party's ticket.

They could do this, of course, only if they held jobs controlled by their own party. It represented their contribution to the party and could be measured in cash value only if one took the amount of their time officially devoted to the campaign and measured it against their public payroll salaries.

In discussion of any party, particularly either of the two major parties, many people are apt to regard the party as consisting entirely of those active in it, rather than those enrolled in it, and base their criticism on that premise. They forget that in the Elks, the Kiwanis, the American Legion, or the Men's League of the First Baptist Church—in any group, no matter how large or small—a few men do the organization's work, for personal glory or satisfaction, hope of recognition or reward. They are the men who wind up running the organization, and while they run it, another group always grumbles about the clique in charge. It is the same in political parties, only on a larger scale. The men who put in the time, effort, and sometimes money run them, and those who join and do nothing else have only themselves to blame.

Chapter V

THE ELEPHANT

Warren T. Thayer, a state Senator representing a group of St. Lawrence River counties, was privately on the payroll of a big up-state public-utility company. He was indiscreet enough at the end of one legislative session to write to his benefactors expressing the hope that his services in handling legislation had been satisfactory to the company. Since Thayer was chairman of the Senate Committee on Public Service, which handled all legislation affecting and regulating utility companies, including his client, there was a first-class scandal when the Federal Trade Commission ran across the letter in the company files.

The Senator resigned, just before he was ousted by his colleagues. The incident was regarded by many as typical of the relationship between the Republican Party and the utility interests of the state. The charge of such a tie-up had been made for years by the Democrats in the course of state campaigns. As a matter of fact, the Thayer incident was neither as typical nor as significant as what happened five years earlier, in 1929, when the big Niagara-Hudson utility holding company was being financed. Then the usual list of insiders, friends of the financiers, were allowed to buy the stock at fifteen dollars a share lower than the price at which it was offered publicly. The favored list on this particular stock issue included everybody who amounted to anything in the GOP. H. Edmund Machold, utility magnate, happened to be Republican state chairman at the time.

The Elephant

A few months after the flotation of the Niagara-Hudson issue the stock market crashed; everybody, including the insiders, lost their shirts, and in the next few years the utility companies lost the control of the state Republican Party, which they had shared with other big-business interests for years. The influence of big business in political affairs sank to its lowest ebb in the early thirties, in the party that traditionally had harkened to its voice.

In the two decades immediately preceding the 1929 boom and crash the Republican Party in the state was run by a group of men who believed sincerely that what was good for big business was good for the people of the state. Unlike Senator Thayer, a lackey of the interests, they were the interests themselves. This was true in many other states at that time, and nationally the men who ran New York had their counterparts in such figures as Nelson Aldrich of Rhode Island, Murray Crane of Massachusetts, and to a lesser extent Hamilton Kean of New Jersey.

In up-state New York many a county chairman was also president of the local bank, owner of the local power company, which grew up from the little generator at the site of the old mill dam and was absorbed later in a state-wide combine, with himself as a big stockholder. He was generally the chief local representative of the established economic order, and as such was also Republican county chairman.

In the state at large it was substantial citizens like Machold and Charles D. Hilles who ran the party up to the 1929 crash. Once they and their predecessors had run the state government, too. From the period of the Civil War to the time of Al Smith they usually elected the Governor and they always controlled the Legislature. Charles Evans Hughes and Teddy Roosevelt got in their hair, but they combed out the trouble and stayed placidly in control.

Starting in the early twenties and continuing through that decade, the Old Guard ran so consistently into diffi-

71

culties in ruling the state that its candidates were handicapped by its label. And like any group that fails to produce an occasional winner, its control of the party was doomed.

There were a number of reasons for the Republicans' conspicuous lack of success in state elections in this period. The Democrats in the same era produced a series of popular vote-getters—Smith, Bob Wagner, James A. Foley, Jimmy Walker—operating under the political genius of Boss Murphy of Tammany Hall. They were vigorous and progressive, in strong contrast with the conservatism of the Old Guard and its lack-luster, stand-pat candidates. The appeal of the opposition party to the young voters was irresistible, and each year, as a new crop came of age, the great majority of them gravitated toward the Democratic rather than the Republican Party. This was especially true in New York City, but even up-state many a good Republican household was upset as one or more of the younger generation turned in his inherited political coat.

In the big city the party got on the black books of the voters particularly because of the five-cent-fare issue. The subways were then privately operated. The owners wanted an increased fare, and the state leadership of the GOP, firm believers in the rights of private enterprise, threw its political support to them. The people were indignant with the inept subway management. Facing a demand that they pay more money for being herded around like cattle, they revolted, staging what amounted to a political lynching bee, with all who favored the fare increase as victims. On this issue alone the Republicans had the ground yanked out from under them for years to come.

Another thing that hurt the Republicans in New York City was prohibition, which the Republicans, being in charge of the national government, had the duty of enforcing. The law was unpopular, particularly with the rising generation, which viewed the eighteenth amendment as an act of national hypocrisy. They saw their officials and law-makers drinking wet but voting dry. The result was that in the state the Republicans sank lower and lower in public esteem, and in the city the preponderance of Democrats over Republicans attained new records.

For a time this applied only to state elections and state issues. The same public that was pleased with Democratic government in the city and the state thought it was doing pretty well with the Republicans running the nation. Warren G. Harding carried New York City in 1920 on a postwar protest vote, but in 1924, when Calvin Coolidge carried every one of the five boroughs, there was another factor at work.

It was "prosperity." Teapot Dome, the Little Green House on K Street, and the unsavory characters from Ohio who floated around in it were forgotten in the belief that business was always good under the Republican Party. In New York City and in up-state cities this was a factor with the small businessman, who also voted for the candidates of Tammany Hall, or the O'Connells in Albany, because he knew he could get a favor done. Those organizations were good for business, too. There also was a substantial group in the then thinner ranks of organized labor that saw merit in the "full dinner-pail" pledge raised by the Republicans, in one form or another, since McKinley's campaign. The Negroes were still for the party that freed them from slavery, and a majority of the Italians was Republican, possibly because of the historical association of the name of the party with that of Garibaldi.

Then came the stock-market crash, and the long depression began. The Republican Hoover administration became whipping-boy for labor and business alike. Republicans who had never believed they could do such a thing voted under the Democratic emblem in 1932. And the New Deal came into full flower, attracting the voters as honey lures the bees. The Republican Party became an empty hive. With its loss of control of the nation, its bankruptcy in leadership and on issues in the state, the party virtually lost its excuse for existence.

Ogden L. Mills and Ruth Baker Pratt, both millionaires, ran the party for Herbert Hoover during the depression years, up to 1933, and while they were estimable persons, they were far from being the leaders the times demanded. When Hoover went out, so did they; but it was too late to avert the revolt against the theory on which the party had been run.

The insurgent movement was led by W. Kingsland Macy, of Suffolk County, who was Republican state chairman because no one else wanted the job. Macy decided that the time was ripe for a change of party control, that the Old Guard grasp had to be pried loose. He chose as his lever the unpopularity of the public utilities. No one was in the public doghouse in those days so completely as the gas and electric companies, with their high rates and watered stock. Macy braved charges of heresy and from his position as nominal head of the party accused it of being run by the interests, particularly the public utilities.

He aimed his fire specifically at the legislative leadership, headed by Speaker Joseph A. McGinnies, and he campaigned against McGinnies's re-election to that post. In the middle of the fight, which Macy was losing, the Thayer letter was disclosed. The public was so outraged that Thayer's colleagues, several of whom were no better than he, found it necessary to vote to remove him from office even after he had resigned. The Old Guard was licked, even though it was able to win a few more battles.

It ousted Macy as state chairman and put up its own nominee for governor that fall, in 1934; but its ticket suffered the worst beating in the history of the state, and Macy won his war. In the next few years there was a shifting of

GOP control, first from the hands of the Old Guard into those of a group of chairmen of the more populous counties, and from their collective grasp into the hands of Tom Dewey.

In that 1934 election the Republican Party, under Old Guard leadership for the last time, lost control of the Legislature. The Democrats elected a majority in both houses. The party was resting on rock bottom. It had no place to go but up, and up it went, steadily for ten years, starting in 1935. That year Kenneth F. Simpson was elected Republican county chairman in New York County. He was a red-haired Irishman, unreliable but brilliant, moody, difficult to get along with, but filled with vigor and imagination.

The first thing Simpson did was to find himself a vote-getting candidate. He picked out Dewey, then special rackets prosecutor in Manhattan. Five minutes before midnight on the night of the legal deadline, he managed to get Dewey to consent to run for district attorney. He had been working on Dewey for many hours and the story at the time, never denied, was that Dewey made his decision to run as he downed his sixteenth Scotch highball. Dewey was elected that fall—his first success at the polls.

In that same campaign year Simpson showed his ability to handle La Guardia, then the Republican Party's problem stepchild. He knew that he had to renominate La Guardia for mayor, on the basis of his record; so he hand-picked from among La Guardia's friends two men to whom La Guardia was beholden but would not choose himself. Simpson named them as La Guardia's running-mates. La Guardia did not dare refuse to take the two, Joe McGoldrick for comptroller and Newbold Morris, and they were elected; but they owed their nomination, and patronage, to Simpson.

The redhead also chiseled out of La Guardia the commitment that the American Labor Party, which La Guardia could then control, would back Republican candidates for delegates to the 1938 state constitutional convention. This step earned Simpson the temporary admiration and gratitude of the party in the entire state, since without those ALP endorsements the GOP would have lost control of the convention. That body, with the Democrats in charge, probably would have been able to put over a new legislative apportionment clause that would have divested the Republicans of their constitutional right to run the Legislature.

So Simpson's stock was high with the other county leaders, like Edwin F. Jaeckle of Erie, J. Russel Sprague of Nassau, William F. Bleakley, the boss if not the chairman in Westchester, Tom Broderick in Monroe, and Clarence King and Rolland B. Marvin in Onondaga.

In 1938, on Simpson's recommendation, they accepted Dewey as the candidate for governor without a murmur. And Dewey, showing remarkable vote-getting power upstate, came within 64,000 votes of winning, compared with the half-million beating the state ticket had absorbed only two years before. Simpson was elected Republican national committeeman, succeeding Hilles. He was close to being state boss. But Simpson was erratic and often arbitrary. Also he made commitments he did not keep. Some began to believe he never intended to keep them. To Dewey, a vote-getter in the eyes of the other leaders, Simpson began to be a liability.

There were a number of incidents. Simpson, at a Washington press conference, said that the party could not ever afford to return to the "days of Hoover." A few days later the stiff-necked former President ignored a hand proffered by Simpson at a social function and stalked off into another room. This was early in 1939, when Dewey was quietly courting Hoover's support for the presidential nomination in 1940. (It turned out later that Hoover desired his own nomination at the Willkie convention.) Dewey decided it would serve his own political career best to break with the man who was his sponsor and publicly accepted spokesman. He chose a dramatic method of renunciation that avoided the embarrassment of a formal statement.

Every year the legislative correspondents in Albany give a stunt dinner of the type made famous nationally by the Gridiron Club. The Albany dinner, oldest of its kind in the country, is attended by every political figure of importance in the state. Afterward there are speeches that may make history, but that may not be reported in the newspapers. At one of those dinners, years before, Charles Evans Hughes, red whiskers shaking, stormed up and down the room, denouncing the leaders of the party that had elected him Governor, threatening to drive them into jail or political oblivion.

Thirty years later Dewey, as a principal speaker, rose and in a calm, almost amused tone, read Simpson, the party's boss, out of Dewey's political life. Dewey said that so far as he was concerned, Simpson could develop "a permanent case of laryngitis." Simpson sat silent, white with rage, as Dewey told the politicians and reporters that Simpson didn't run him any more. The most interesting feud in the history of the party was born. The first development was that the other county leaders, by then down on Simpson, turned eagerly to Dewey as their standard-bearer and rallying-point, as the man they could best use to oust Simpson from the position of power he had attained. At the request of the bosses back home, a public statement was issued by the legislative leaders, announcing that in matters of state policy they would listen to Dewey's advice. Dewey himself laid plans to oust Simpson that fall as chairman of New York County.

Simpson, who was no more tactful in handling his county district leaders in Manhattan than he was in dealing with the other county chairmen, could have been ousted if Dewey had actually taken the leadership in a fight against him. But Simpson started a backfire. With the reputation nationally of being a liberal, he had friends make speeches on the floor of Congress; he had letters written from various sections of the country, all asking if Dewey was turning conservative and playing with the Old Guard against the man who had liberalized the party in New York. Simpson's hand never showed publicly, but Dewey understood, and recognized he was engaging a dangerous opponent.

He made a peace offer. Under it, Dewey would—and did —support Simpson for re-election as county chairman, if the latter promised to support Dewey for president in 1940 for as long during the convention as Dewey was a "serious contender." Dewey took that commitment at face value. Simpson did not. In his eyes, Dewey could never be a "serious contender."

After his re-election as county chairman, and with the prestige of his national committee membership behind him, he spread word around the country that Dewey would not have solid backing from his own state at the convention. Dewey got 360 votes on the first ballot at Philadelphia, but only 61 of the 93 from New York. Simpson early swung his support to Willkie, and Willkie was nominated. But the Dewey forces, aided by the continuing alliance of anti-Simpson county leaders, kicked Simpson out as national committeeman at that same convention, and his ouster as county chairman would have followed, no doubt; but Simpson died shortly after he had been elected to Congress from his own district.

The battle for state delegates waged by the Dewey forces at the Philadelphia convention produced one of the most amusing of all convention stories. One delegate, to whom the party owed eight thousand dollars, the Dewey managers wanted on their side because of his prominence. When approached, he indicated he might be favorable, but asked what about the eight thousand dollars. Dewey's representatives hustled out and borrowed it. Then one cautious soul suggested they might play it safe—give him half before the balloting and half afterward. But no one had the nerve to put that up to the delegate; they gave him the eight thousand dollars, and he voted for Willkie.

From the time of Willkie's defeat in the election and Simpson's death shortly after, no real obstacle remained to Dewey's domination of the party. He tied up tighter and tighter his alliances with the chairmen of the big counties and he was unopposed for the nomination for governor at the party's Saratoga convention in 1942. It is not generally known that in the spring of that year, when Dewey loomed as the certain nominee of his party, Willkie had similar aspirations. They were logical enough. One of Willkie's handicaps in 1940 was that he had had no experience in governmental office. He felt that if he could be elected governor of New York in 1942, he would have the experience and additional prestige by the time the 1944 convention rolled around.

But Willkie's dilemma was that he did not dare make a bid for the nomination that would be unsuccessful. A defeat for the gubernatorial nomination in his adopted state would eliminate any chances he had for renomination for the Presidency, he felt. And in a fight for state convention delegates Dewey, aided by the county machines, would be sure to win. So Willkie put the quietus on a draft movement started by friends, and contented himself with lecturing the party on the desirability of nominating someone other than Dewey. At the legislative correspondents' dinner in 1942 already mentioned, he gave the audience a description of the man he felt the party should *not* nominate for governor. It was unflattering, and everyone present, including Dewey, knew whom Willkie was portraying. Later Willkie publicly named a list of twelve acceptable nominees, none of whom was Dewey. Leaving aside his own ambitions, Willkie sincerely opposed Dewey in the belief that the latter was not sufficiently international-minded. He foresaw that Dewey's election as governor would lead to his nomination for the Presidency, and such an occurrence did not fit into Willkie's One World concept.

But the leaders in the state felt that Dewey would be good for them and for the party, and they were right. More than any other one man he built up the party organization to a high point of power and efficiency. The Republicans who were willing to go along with Dewey—and eventually this meant everyone occupying party position or public office—were rewarded with ample state patronage, in the form of jobs and the ability to secure favors for their constituents.

Probably state patronage has never been used more intelligently and to greater effect than by Dewey to keep his party in line and to put his policies into effect. Those few who opposed him were put into the political ash-can with neatness and dispatch. Rolland B. Marvin of Syracuse had supported Willkie in 1940, before the balloting began in Philadelphia, and he remained tied to Willkie by bonds of personal affection. Dewey cut off his state patronage, set up a rival dispenser in Marvin's home town, and sat back and waited for the local organization to unseat Marvin, as it did in short order. A political leader who can't deliver jobs or favors when they are to be had is always doomed to early death. A number of others, none so prominent as Marvin, likewise disappeared from the public ken, for the same reason.

But Sprague of Nassau, who became national committeeman and chief lieutenant for Dewey, fared very well, as did Broderick of Monroe, a convert to the Dewey standard. Westchester and Suffolk leaders, the Dutchess and Erie organizations, may have grumbled quietly over the bows they had to make to the supreme authority in the party, but they never could complain about the political pay-offs.

One of the phenomena of the times which contributed to the resurgence of the Republican Party under Dewey was the growth of the party's vote in the suburban counties surrounding New York City, particularly Nassau and Westchester. These counties had always been Republican, but for years they had been drawing their increased population from people moving out of New York City, a majority of them Democrats. Some feared that the old Republican vote in these counties would eventually be overrun. If there was such a trend in the making, it was checked in the Dewey era by three factors.

One of these is the tendency of people moving into an area to be assimilated by the dominant political organization. Unless they have strong political convictions, they find themselves going with the tide, first on local candidates, later on major issues. The second, which ties in with the first, stems from the type of government given by the local organization. The Republican machines in these counties were run efficiently and furnished good, though political, local government. The third reason was that Dewey had a definite appeal as Governor to the upper middle class, from which he came. He had strength among the people who could afford to take their children out of the crowded city, who could buy surburban homes and pay commutation fares, or drive to work in their own cars. The suburban majorities for the GOP climbed higher and higher.

The increased suburban vote was needed to replace the strictly rural vote on which the GOP had once relied. Here is a story about the dependability of the rural vote. Lou Payne, a political boss of the Hudson River valley counties years ago, was riding across the state on the observation platform of a train with a political celebrity from another state. As they passed a cemetery, the visiting fireman remarked that he had heard the GOP voted the tombstones whenever it could get away with it. "That's true sometimes,' Payne mused, "but you should know we never vote a man unless he would have voted our way if he were still alive. We respect a man's convictions."

Possibly fraud became more difficult as the years went on. In any event, the tombstone vote became less and less important. Weak up-state Republican organizations found it harder and harder to induce even the live farmers to go to the polls. Under Dewey, steps were once more taken to exploit to the fullest advantage the naturally Republican farm vote, even though the number of farmers had lessened. The state Farm Bureau system was used in the 1946 election the same way the Democrats used the Agricultural Adjustment Administration machinery in the 1936 election for Roosevelt. The principal farmer on a road, the man who owned the machinery his neighbors borrowed or rented, was made a captain in charge of his neighbors' votes.

He was to convert them if necessary—a rare thing—but more importantly he was to see that they got to the polls on election day. Baby-sitters were furnished for farm wives; every county organization was held responsible for getting out the votes surveyed by Dewey's council of war. Analysis of the rural vote in the 1946 election, the first time this intensive drive was made, seemed to indicate that it had netted the Republicans upwards of 100,000 voters who might otherwise have stayed at home.

Dewey's tactics were often rough in the handling of individuals and they caused resentment here and there in the party structure; but there never was any open revolt. The basis for this surface loyalty was expressed years ago, in entirely different circumstances, by the same Lou Payne mentioned above. Undisputed boss of his area, he walked into a conference of other leaders who were waiting for him to tell them who the congressional candidate would be.

Payne, late for the meeting, wasted no more of their time and gave them the name.

One of the other leaders, aghast, said: "Lou, you know anything you say goes, but isn't he the guy you've been going up and down your county calling a blankety blank blank blank?"

Payne replied: "Sure, that's the guy. But I just left his house after a two-hour talk—that's why I was late—and from now on he's *my* blankety blank blank blank."

The influence of Dewey in and on the Republican Party has been, as noted, tremendous. However, for a period of about five years before he assumed the Governorship another group of men also did very effective work. They were the leaders of the Legislature, and of the Assembly in particular, who by 1937 had taken over important posts vacated by Old Guard retirements: Speaker Oswald D. Heck, Majority Leader Irving M. Ives, Ways and Means Chairman Abbot Low Moffat. All were in their middle thirties at the time and they shared, in addition to youth, a common desire to do a good job. In the five years between 1937 and 1942 they wiped off the label of obstructionism that their predecessors had caused to be attached to their party and its legislative majorities. When they did oppose the program of the Democratic Governor, they usually offered a positive program of their own as a substitute. Ives rewrote the state's labor-relations act in a typical middle-of-the-road manner; Moffat set up a legislative fiscal program in opposition to that of the Governor; Heck preserved harmony among the membership and fended off political interference from the outside as much as he could. The triumvirate for a time made GOP policy in the state. They had the co-operation in the Senate first of Perley A. Pitcher and later of Joe R. Hanley, and they remained in command of the party on Capitol Hill until Dewey took office as Governor. By the start of Dewey's second term only Speaker Heck remained.

Moffat quit early, in disgust, to enter the foreign service. Ives retired to the deanship of the School of Labor and Industrial Relations he had founded at Cornell, and then went to the United States Senate. Hanley was promoted to the Lieutenant-Governorship. They were succeeded in the Legislature by Mallory Stephens, Lee B. Mailler, and Benjamin F. Feinberg, respectively, all able men, but with the scope of their work and authority curtailed sharply by the Executive Office exactly the way the Democratic leadership on the Hill in Washington was crimped during the days of Roosevelt's domination of Congress.

The legislative leadership did not lose all its influence, however. It was able to persuade Dewey to accept Ives for the senatorial nomination in 1946. Ives had wanted the nomination in 1944, before he retired to Cornell, but Dewey decided he needed a Catholic on the ticket as a running-mate, and he picked Thomas J. Curran, the New York County Republican chairman. Curran was beaten by Robert F. Wagner, just as Dewey was beaten for the Presidency that year by Roosevelt. By 1946, when a second Senate contest was to be waged, Ives, out of the Legislature, was still willing to run, but would not lift a hand to get himself the nomination.

Friends of William J. Donovan, head of the wartime Office of Strategic Services, started a Donovan boom. For reasons never made clear, Dewey flatly opposed Donovan's candidacy and tried to head it off by picking Hugh A. Drum, a retired general who headed the State Guard.

Even though the Governor was boss, the Drum candidacy proved hard to put over, and Dewey found himself sorely in need of another candidate. Heck, Stephens, and Hanley stepped in and persuaded Dewey that their friend Ives was the man; even though not a Catholic, he fitted every other requirement. The Governor's office obtained what it believed to be assurances that the lack of a Catholic on the ticket would not be resented, and Ives was nominated and elected.

The election of a Republican United States Senator in 1946 was particularly significant of the progress made by the party, for the last one elected had been James W. Wadsworth in 1920. It seemed to indicate that the Republicans were becoming, if only for a few years, the majority party in the state in fact as well as in theory. The party had achieved the majority position, technically, after the 1938 election, since the election law provides that the party polling the largest number of votes for its candidate for governor is the majority party and is entitled to the first position on the voting machine for its candidates. In 1938 the vote for Dewey on the Republican line was larger than the vote for Lehman on the Democratic line (Lehman gained his election from the ALP votes). The Republicans moved into first place and Edwin F. Jaeckle, the Republican state chairman, called it a "moral victory" for his party.

He was laughed at then, and again when he repeated the remark in 1940, the second election in a row in which the Republicans polled the most votes as an individual group but still lost the election. After the election of 1946 the Democrats stopped laughing.

Chapter VI

THE DONKEY

The newspapermen in the State Capitol in Albany were reluctant to interrupt their press-room rummy game that morning, but a couple of the boys from New York City papers had asked for a press conference with the Governor, to see what he was going to do about "the Bronx paving-block scandal" and it wasn't polite to let only a corporal's guard attend. They all liked Herbert Lehman, the practically perpetual Governor, even though he seldom furnished them with any startling news, so they put the decks aside and sauntered down at the appointed time to the Executive Offices on the second floor. A couple were heard to grumble over the waste of time.

In less than three minutes they came running back up, shouting for telegraph and telephone lines. Their bulletins became headlines for the noon editions, as fast as the news could be transmitted and set in type. Lehman had handed them a terse statement declaring that under no circumstances would he run again for governor that fall. He had done that once four years earlier, but this time everyone knew it would stick, and the newspapermen felt that an era had come to an end.

They were right. The statement itself and the circumstances under which it was issued brought to a close the Democratic dynasty in New York State that had started with Smith and had continued through Roosevelt and Lehman. It marked finis to an era of unequaled govern-

86

mental progress under one party and it started the opposition GOP on an upward swing.

All this happened on a spring morning in 1942, but in order to understand the impact of the 1942 campaign and election on the political history of the state it is necessary first to go back to the previous gubernatorial election, in 1938. That was the year the Republicans first nominated Dewey for governor. He was fresh from his successful rackets investigation in New York County, he was free from any identification as a professional politician; his armor was bright and shining. The Democrats took one look at him and knew he was the nearest thing to a winning candidate that the Republicans had named in years. Then they looked around to see whom they had to oppose him—someone other than Lehman, known to be unwilling to run.

To the complete surprise of the Democratic state leadership, they had no sure winner, as they always had had in the past. They were just "fresh out" of candidates. Not enough attention had been paid to building for the future. Jim Farley, the state chairman, had tried, it was true, to build up Robert Jackson of Jamestown, later a Justice of the United States Supreme Court, but the Jackson boom did not click. Farley himself was urged by Roosevelt to run, but refused. Lehman went to the Rochester convention of the party that fall determined not to subject himself to another term as head of the state government. His determination was strengthened by the fact that the term had just been lengthened from two to four years.

But Lehman was the only man in sight who looked like a winner against Dewey, and the pressure the party leaders applied was terrific. They passed through the Governor's hotel suite in relays. The professional politicians stressed the party's need for him, and then teams of social workers and labor leaders, following up, pictured to him the dismal fate of the reform legislation of the previous two decades if turned over to a Republican state administration. The Governor gave in—consented to run. In the campaign that followed, Dewey, armed with the racket-investigation data from Manhattan and charges of vote frauds against the O'Connell machine in Albany, portrayed Lehman as the front for a corrupt state-wide Democratic machine. Lehman ran on his record and won.

By 1942 the nation was at war. In the spring of that year it looked as if Dewey had lost some of his freshness and appeal as a political figure. He was out of office, his connections with the war effort was limited to chairmanship of the USO drive, he had last figured in the public eye as a defeated aspirant for the presidential nomination in 1940. He controlled his party's organization and was its predestined nominee for governor, but potentially he was many thousands of votes weaker than he had been in 1938. Meanwhile Lehman had been giving hints of his own revised position. He told members of his kitchen cabinet that no man had the right to leave office in the middle of a war, that the home-front job was important. He made two cabinet appointments, M. William Bray of Utica to the Public Service Commission and John Splain of Queens as Motor Vehicle Commissioner, both purely political nominations, designed to strengthen his own hand.

A hint, in negative form, was given me as head of the legislative bureau of the *New York Times.* In 1938, at the start of the legislative session, I had asked Mr. Lehman, for confidential background purposes, whether he intended to run again. His answer in 1938 was: "I cannot now conceive of any set of circumstances that would induce me to again be a candidate for Governor." But in 1942, when the question was asked again, and on the same basis, the Governor declined to answer. He gave the appearance, to those on the inside, of being a man who felt he had to continue in office whether he wanted to or not.

Then the Bronx paving-block scandal made newspaper headlines. It consisted in an accusation that Edward J. Flynn, the Bronx boss, a successful lawyer and wealthier than any other county leader in the state, had used a few hundred dollars' worth of city property and city labor to refurbish a courtyard on his country estate. Actually the only way the affair came to light was when Flynn, discovering what had been done in his behalf, made arrangements to pay for it, and Mayor La Guardia approved. But the matter leaked out in a different form and the newspapers pressed for action of some kind. That was how the press conference with the Governor came to be set, how the morning card-game was broken up.

The statement the Governor handed out did not deal with the subject for which the conference had been called. The paving-blocks were never mentioned in reporters' haste to catch editions with the bigger news. The interference is there that Lehman made up his mind suddenly—that the accusation of being a "front" made by Dewey in 1938 still rankled and he did not want to subject himself to it again in 1942.

This much is known: the Governor consulted not a single party leader in advance of his announcement; it was prepared the night before it was issued and only two of his closest advisers were told of what he was going to do; then they were asked for approval of form, not content. There was no chance for a round-table discussion of who his successor might be.

Up to that time President Roosevelt had been quietly pushing Owen D. Young as a possibility if Lehman retired. Jim Farley, by then in Roosevelt's political doghouse, felt he could stay important in politics only if he retained control of the New York State situation by picking and electing a governor. Farley would have made a good candidate himself. Even though he had opposed the third term for

Roosevelt in 1940, he was personally popular, and the American Labor Party, thoroughly pro-Roosevelt, was nevertheless prepared to give Farley its endorsement if he would run for governor on the Democratic ticket. But he wasn't interested for himself. He had his candidate in the person of John J. Bennett, Jr., the state's Attorney General. Farley, however, could not even seek delegates to support Bennett as long as Lehman was a possible candidate for re-election.

Had Lehman called the party chiefs into a quiet conference and told them he wanted to quit but would not unless they could agree on a successor who could be elected, the mess that followed might have been avoided. But instead the party leaders learned of the Governor's decision from the newspapers.

Farley immediately went to work on the telephone and before nightfall had a majority of the county chairmen and delegates pledged to support him in the Bennett drive. He never lost that majority, either. Farley could do this over the telephone because of the years of personal contact he had had with every county chairman, with almost everybody scheduled to be a convention delegate. The White House and the Governor's office, far removed from the scene, had no such intimate contacts.

Farley's tactics were perfect; his only, but fatal error lay in himself not running. Bennett, a really capable Attorney General, was not the man to head the ticket. To the public at large he did not seem to be in the Smith-Roosevelt-Lehman tradition. He had other handicaps, too. Labor viewed him with suspicion, unjustified but important, because he had been an early organizer of the American Legion, and Legion posts had lent themselves to strike-breaking in the days following World War I. As a good Catholic, he had presided five years before at a meeting designed to raise funds for medical relief for the Franco forces in Spain. Thus he went into the campaign labeled "anti-labor" and "Fascist," neither charge correct.

The leaders of the American Labor Party, hitherto allied with the Democrats in state and national campaigns, revolted against the pending nomination of Bennett by the Democratic organizations and took their case directly to President Roosevelt. They were the second to do so.

Farley had been there first. He had told the President that he controlled the votes to nominate Bennett at the party convention and what he wanted to know was whether the President would support Bennett in the election. The President told Farley of his own friendship for Bennett in such terms that Farley believed it meant a commitment of support. The President did eventually, a few days before election, make an appeal for Bennett, but this was after he had opposed him for the nomination, so the belated blessing publicly bestowed was meaningless.

The American Labor Party leaders on their trip to Washington convinced the President that he should not support Bennett for the nomination. With White House approval, a move to block Farley's candidate by nominating James M. Mead, the junior Senator from the state, was launched instead. Mead was never the real candidate of the Roosevelt forces in 1942; he was just the man and the name they used to try to head off the Bennett movement. It became a test of strength within the state, a battle Farley felt he had to win, and Farley would never consent to a switch, to a compromise. Bennett was nominated at a Brooklyn convention where the Roosevelt forces were outvoted on a roll-call and where some Bennett supporters, far too enthusiastic for their candidate's good, booed the names of Roosevelt and Lehman, their party's top men in the state and nation.

The election was over, then and there—Dewey was in. If there had never been a fight within the party, the Demo-

91

crats, with a candidate on whom the party could unite, would have won another election, would have continued the series that started so far back. They could have won with Lehman, Farley, or Young. They might even have won with Charles Poletti, Lehman's young Lieutenant Governor, who consented to run for that office again on the Bennett ticket and came within 50,000 votes of election even though Dewey won by 650,000. Poletti had the nomination of the ALP as well as of the Democratic Party, while Bennett ran on the Democratic ticket alone. The ALP, then under right-wing control, put up a separate candidate for Governor—Dean Alfange—and polled 403,000 votes for him. Dewey received an actual majority over the combined vote for Bennett and Alfange, but this was owing to the fact that a large segment of the New Deal, Roosevelt voters in New York City voted for Dewey doubly to insure Bennett's defeat and Farley's chastisement. Poletti, it might be noted, shortly afterward jeopardized a very promising political career by an injudicious pardon issued to an arsonist during the thirty-day period he was Governor, following Lehman's resignation in November 1942.

Farley had gambled and lost on the Bennett nomination, and his influence dwindled from that time on. For the two years he remained thereafter as state chairman, the national administration continued to ignore him on patronage, and the state machinery had passed into Republican hands.

To show to what depths the Democratic Party sunk after the 1942 defeat, one might point to the campaign to elect a lieutenant governor the following year. Reporters found the luckless candidate answering mail himself while his campaign manager tended the telephone switchboard.

It had not helped the party to allow Farley to continue as state chairman from 1940, when he openly broke with Roosevelt and resigned as national chairman, through 1944. He had no interest in the fortunes of the New Deal, and the

New Dealers none in his. In addition, and more important, the state party machinery had been geared for years to rely on research facilities provided by the departments of the state government, on data they furnished, on manpower they supplied. The legislative leadership was in the same position. When the Democrats lost the Governorship, their political agencies were left as clean as if they had lost the last bet in a table-stakes poker game.

Roosevelt's own vote-getting capacity, plus his status as wartime commander-in-chief, pulled the party through the 1944 election without difficulty, but it was no go in 1946 when Dewey came up for re-election as Governor. The times were bad for the Democrats anyhow, but they were also weary, discouraged, and poverty-stricken, in leadership and candidates, and that is not the kind of party that wins elections.

It was a far cry from the past. From the end of the Civil War to the end of World War I the Republicans had elected more Governors than the Democrats in the state, but the latter were always in the running. From 1918 on through 1942 the Democrats lost the office only once, in the Harding national landslide of 1920. Al Smith had started off the modern run of successes, squeezing through by fewer than 15,000 votes, including soldier ballots, in the 1918 election.

Political observers of that era still contend that Smith would have been defeated by Charles S. Whitman—the Dewey of his day—if Whitman, running for a third term as Governor, had not been campaigning as a political "dry" while showing himself to be personally "wet." The prohibition issue was important in those days; it was also the first election in which women voted in the state. Whitman's obvious bibulousness on an up-state tour did not appeal to the segment of the electorate that favored the abolition of the saloon. This was before the days of cocktail lounges.

However, Smith, elected, made a fine record in his first

93

term, and even though he went down, with every other Democrat, in the 1920 catastrophe, his own personal stock increased in defeat. He ran a million votes ahead of the national ticket of James M. Cox and Franklin D. Roosevelt in his home state and he came bouncing back in the election of 1922 to win a second term as Governor by a then record majority. It was twenty years before the party he headed again faced the loss of power.

The party that Smith headed was not really a state-wide one. Virtually its entire organization and nearly all of its votes were in New York City. Albany was just beginning to feel Democratic growing-pains with the up and coming O'Connell clan about to kick out the old Barnes machine. The rest of the cities of the state were Republican, and there were discernible signs of Democratic strength in only four or five rural counties. In New York City, though Tammany was then as now the official organization only in New York County, its influence still ran the Bronx, which had become a separate county only a few years before.

The Mayor, "Red Mike" Hylan, came from Brooklyn, but the Brooklyn organization, under John H. McCooey, was content to follow the lead of Murphy of Tammany on city and state matters. Queens and Richmond were completely unimportant political appendages. Murphy was the real boss, Smith the magnet for the voters, and their interests never clashed. Smith left the political leadership to Murphy and built up his personal following among Republicans and independents who were willing to trust him with the running of the state even if they trusted no other machine Democrat. The Smith hold on the voters became catching, though. They started voting for Al and his brown derby and found it easier and easier as the years went by to vote also for the party he headed.

After Murphy died, Smith exercised the political leadership which fell into his lap by booting out Hylan as the party's Mayor. Hylan was inept, bumbling, and much too close to William Randolph Hearst, whom Smith hated, so Hylan had to go. Smith offered the nomination first to James A. Foley, who declined, second to Bob Wagner, who shied away.

Jimmy Walker, Smith's third choice, accepted. He defeated Hylan in a city-wide primary fight and coasted into the mayoralty in the fall election in 1925. The party rose to the height of its power and at the same time started greasing the skids for its slide down. Politicians who look back at it now agree that its return to disrepute in local affairs was mostly Jimmy Walker's fault. He was one of the most charming men ever to hold public office. Everybody loved him and nobody could ever stay angry with him. He could have done anything he wanted to with the party and the city. Jimmy was careless, however, in his morals, his habits, and the hours he kept, and he had a live-and-let-live attitude that forgave far too many sins.

Tammany, which had been a careful, not too grasping machine under Murphy, went completely on the loose. Walker's own carelessness and don't-give-a-damn behavior set the tone. Even the elementary principles of caution were forgotten. The boys stole and stole, and forgot to give the city much in the way of government in return. Crime was protected, corruption was a commonplace. The gay larceny parade eventually marched under the floodlights of the Seabury investigation, and before it was over, Walker was an exile and the party was out of power in New York City for twelve years.

In New York County the boys stole enough votes in the 1933 election to keep control of the District Attorney's office, but all that served to do was to bring about the Dewey rackets investigation of 1935, because the Tammany prosecutor's office couldn't somehow get any convictions of underworld characters who had helped put the prosecutor in office.

Though the city Democrats dropped to low levels of public esteem in the early thirties, it was also true that the voters made a distinction between them and the state-wide leaders of the party. The city voters went overwhelmingly for Roosevelt for President and Lehman for Governor in 1932, in the middle of the whole Walker scandal; they elected La Guardia Mayor the next year to punish Tammany for its misdeeds, and turned around the following year to give Lehman a new record majority for re-election to the Governorship.

Tammany, of course, made it easy for the voters. It opposed Roosevelt for nomination for president and lost; it opposed Lehman for the nomination for governor and lost. A whole series of well-publicized and ineffectual gestures by the organization kept the public constantly aware of the fact that it could vote for Roosevelt and Lehman and still not be for Tammany. Tammany needed a thorough reorganization, but the only one who could do it was a Democratic mayor armed with the City Hall patronage, so nothing much was done by anyone about that organization until the end of the La Guardia rule in City Hall, and the entrance into big-time politics of William O'Dwyer. The election of O'Dwyer came in 1945, after the war, after the death of Roosevelt, and in the midst of a general public let-down. If his election had required any great effort or genius on the part of the Democratic political machines in the city, it possibly would not have occurred. But it was a pushover in advance, so he won.

The organizations throughout the state were in bad shape generally. Up-state, Democratic machines had come into being in virtually all of the cities, but they were used to relying on vigorous leadership from Roosevelt on matters of government and from Farley on matters of politics, and they were left stranded in the immediate postwar period.

In New York City the local Democrats regained control of City Hall with the advent of O'Dwyer, but it was nothing like the control they had had before. In the first place, county sinecures had been wiped out by the reorganization of county governments forced by La Guardia. Secondly, many important city posts were occupied by men holding definite terms of office. For example, every magistrate on the bench owed his position, not to the Democratic organizations, but to La Guardia, since Fiorello had been in for twelve years and the term of a magistrate is ten. No one before La Guardia's time had ever figured on a reform administration succeeding itself, and while the machines had been able to stand his first four years in office, with their carry-over appointees, the last eight years were ruinous.

In addition, there was O'Dwyer himself, who displayed from the start every intention of running the show himself, with political benefits to the organizations incidental rather than being distributed to fatten them. He used whatever patronage he gave them to reform, rather than reward, the various county organizations.

O'Dwyer had no difficulties with the relatively clean Flynn organization in the Bronx, and he was able, through his patronage, to force the Brooklyn organization to pick a leader—John Cashmore—acceptable to him when Frank V. Kelly died. But he also found the Queens and Tammany groups asking many privileges that he could not conscientiously grant and sending him too many job-holders who got into trouble and had to be fired. O'Dwyer, at least at the start, was trying to run an honest city government, along the lines drawn by La Guardia, only more tolerant of orthodox politics. Some of the old machine boys did not understand.

Another group of his original supporters with whom he

had under-cover trouble were the Communists functioning within the American Labor Party. They were all for him and for political unity through the 1945 campaign, but about that time Russian foreign policy went into a rapid reverse, dissension rather than co-operation became their menu of the day throughout the world, and it showed up in things as local and mundane as the New York City Council, where the ALP and the Commies had four out of twenty-three members under the proportional system of representation then in effect. O'Dwyer pulled farther and farther away from them.

Tied up with O'Dwyer's decisions to veer away from the ultra-radical political movements in the city was his decision also to reorganize Tammany Hall. Tammany was always "practical," and in the course of being practical it had got itself, the oldest Irish-Catholic political organization in the world, tied up with the Communists. The key men in the alliance were Clarence H. Neal and Bert Stand for Tammany, and Vito Marcantonio, county chairman of the ALP for the left-wingers.

Marcantonio, who started out in political life as a Republican and who wound up with an almost but not quite perfect record of adherence to the Communist party line, functioned up in Harlem. He was a protégé of La Guardia, and during the La Guardia administration was given privileges by the Mayor that the Little Flower would never have dreamed of permitting elsewhere. Marcantonio was the only leader in the city capable of giving out certain kinds of favors, and he gave them out to Republicans and Democrats, too. He built up a patronage machine unequaled in the city, and working for him were many men who were actually district leaders and district captains in both major parties. In addition, he was highly intelligent and full of energy, constantly helping his constituents and also preaching collective benefits to the poorest people of the city, the "spiggoty" population of East Harlem, Negroes, Puerto Ricans. The accusation that he was a Communist hurt him little in an area where capitalism showed so few of its own virtues.

Stand, the secretary of Tammany, and Neal, chairman of its committee on elections, made an even closer alliance with "Marc," as he was known, than any of the Republican leaders in the area, though Marc had started out as a Republican. Twice they gave him their party's designation for Congress, and with local GOP help he captured the Republican primary too and went before his constituents as the nominee of the three principal parties, unopposed in the general election.

In 1946 the Neal-Stand leadership of Tammany gave Marcantonio the designation for Congress and the Republicans in the area would have remained quiescent had not the party's state leadership demanded an on-the-level fight against him in the GOP primary. Marc probably would have won both contests had not Marshal Tito in Jugoslavia started shooting down American pilots a few days before the primary election, making anyone even vaguely connected with Communism very unpopular. Marc lost the Republican primary and squeaked through the Democratic one only as a result of all the help the Democratic machine could give him.

The real explosion came on election day, when Marcantonio won. A Republican election district captain, Joseph Scottoriggio, was beaten to death by a couple of plug-uglies while on his way to the polls. Undoubtedly they intended only to see that he didn't reach the polls and make a nuisance of himself, since he was of the type who couldn't be bought off, but they overdid the beating. It was the first election killing in New York in decades and the newspaper reaction was tremendous.

It was following this that O'Dwyer served notice that the Neal-Stand leadership of Tammany, with its Marcantonio alliance, had to go, and by use of the patronage power of City Hall he finally swung enough of the Tammany executive committee to his side to elect Frank J. Sampson as leader.

Another major development was the passage of the Wilson-Pakula law by the 1947 session of the state Legislature, under which a candidate was limited to entering the primary of the party in which he was enrolled and could enter another primary as a contestant for the nomination only with the consent of the county committee—that is, the organization—of the other party. It was aimed primarily at Marcantonio, but the effect was to end "raiding" of one party's primary by the candidate of another, a practice that had grown more common in recent years.

A further refinement of the law, also aimed at the then existing alliance between the Democratic and the American Labor parties, provided that a man could not accept a second nomination by default. He could no longer tell the public that he wasn't responsible for whatever group chose to support him. He was required, by a section slipped quietly into the election law, to signify his acceptance, in writing, of any nomination given to him by a party of which he was not a member. This meant, for 1948, that the Democratic Party presidential electors, all forty-seven of them, would have had to sign acceptances of ALP nominations to get the support that previously had been given to them without action on their part. It was one of the factors that made the Democrats decide they would not take ALP support in 1948 even if proffered, a decision that proved unnecessary in view of the Wallace candidacy.

From 1946 on, the swing within the Democratic Party against the "Communists" was rapid and violent. Using the Truman doctrine as a lever, the party chiefs rapidly cast off groups with which they formerly had accepted alliances. First in the Bronx and later in Brooklyn, Democratic candidates began refusing to accept nominations offered by the American Labor Party while accepting those given by the Liberal Party, more conservative offshoot of the former.

There were those who worried about the fate of the Democratic Party in the nation, back in 1928, when Al Smith went down to defeat for the Presidency and lost the electoral votes of four of the states in the South that had never voted Republican before. Similarly there were Democrats who, in the years following 1942 and their loss of state control, worried about the fate of the Democratic Party in the state, wondering when and how it would become the majority party again.

Those who now feel such concern should remember that the party has never been a homogeneous one, even in its days of success, and still it would come bouncing back from defeat. Also, it has been a well-financed party. It had big-business support at the start of this century from men like Thomas Fortune Ryan and August Belmont; it had wealthy supporters like the Lehman and Morgenthau families in the days of Al Smith and Roosevelt. Today it has many others who will give time and money to support its nominees. It may lose the 1948 election, and even the state election that follows in 1950, but the odds favor its coming back to control in the state some time after that, just as it did in the nation after the dark years between 1920 and 1928.

Chapter VII

THE SPLINTER PARTIES

Splinter parties" is a term lifted from the political scene abroad and applied to the groups operating in New York State to the political left of the Democratic Party. One of Tom Dewey's anonymous but talented ghost-writers gave the phrase its widest circulation in the 1946 campaign, when the most important of these groups, the American Labor Party, was just ten years old. It seemed appropriate, since the American Labor Party was perpetually threatened with a split between left and right wings, the Liberal Party was itself a right-wing offshoot of the ALP, and support of both had sprung at least in part from the Democratic Party.

The old Socialist Party still put up candidates for public office, but exercised no influence. The Communist Party, theoretically away off to the far corner of the political left by itself, was actually functioning within the ALP.

The American Labor Party was founded to help implement the political aims of Franklin D. Roosevelt. The Liberal Party was committed to the same goal. Both attracted to their standards large groups of independent voters not satisfied with the political machinery furnished by the Republicans and the Democrats. Yet they were more often than not embroiled in internecine warfare, which limited their effectiveness. The principal reason lay in the activity of the Communists.

The largest number of votes the Communists ever polled in New York State was 107,000, rolled up for a candidate for Representative at Large in the 1938 election, in which 4,750,000 persons voted. Even when the electorate was much smaller, the old Socialist Party had attracted several times as many votes for a good candidate. Thus the Commies were not really strong in New York when the American Labor Party was started, and yet any discussion of that group and its offshoots must start and wind up with the Commies. They hovered around like a discarded suitor at the wedding of the ALP and the Democrats, bided their time during the early years of the marriage, and were quick to jump in at the first sign of a spat.

The Republicans and the anti-New Deal Democrats began crying wolf about the Communist influence in the American Labor Party as early as 1936, when the party was born. It should be recorded that Communist influence was then nonexistent; the quiet penetration and infiltration that later led to control had not yet begun.

The men who founded the American Labor Party were bitter Communist-haters. Their hate was of the informed kind based on intimate knowledge and experience. These men were David Dubinsky of the International Ladies Garment Workers Union, the late Sidney Hillman of the Amalgamated Clothing Workers, Jacob Potofsky, Hyman Blumberg, and Luigi Antonini, also of the garment-trades unions, and Alex Rose of the Millinery Workers.

There were also some old-time Socialists like Louis Waldman and Charles Solomon, veteran Communist-haters.

To understand the bitterness of the trade-union leaders, it is necessary to go back another decade, to 1926, the year of the big strike in the needle-trades industry. At that time, after years of painstaking work and skillful agitation, the Commies had gained control of the garment-industry unions. Hillman and Dubinsky, who had brought their unions to greatness by welfare work and straight labor-organizing tactics, had lost control of local union after local union.

They were on the sidelines when the Communist leadership, for militant revolutionary rather than unionist aims, called an industry-wide strike.

It turned out to be a losing strike. After dragging on and on for months, the unions settled for small gains that they could have obtained from the employers without losing a single day's pay. The Communists lost prestige, and Hillman and Dubinsky and their lieutenants started a comeback.

The war that followed was bitter and bloody. Each side hired thugs. The Communists used a batch of gunmen lent them by the late Arnold Rothstein, the gambler whose death in the Park Central Hotel is still one of New York's unsolved mysteries. The right-wing leadership found even less pleasant characters allied with it—Louis Buchalter and Jacob Shapiro (Lepke and Gurrah) and their thugs. That marked, incidentally, the entrance of the latter two into big-time racketeering.

Brought in to do battle with the Commies, they retained a foothold in the garment industry until they went to the electric chair and jail, respectively. Before Lepke and his boys won the battle with the Commies, skulls were cracked, mayhem and murder committed. The Reds did retain control of the unions in the fur industry for the simple reason that the Communist furriers, with their machete-like cutting hooks, implements of their trade, were tougher than Lepke's gorillas, who used only brass knuckles and .45's.

It was these same garment-trades unions, headed by men who'd rather see a Communist dead than running one of their unions, that rallied to the call that came in 1936 for organized labor to support Franklin D. Roosevelt for a second term as President. The appeal, which was timely, came originally from the President himself. He thought it would be a good idea to have labor and white-collar independent voters organize as a political arm of the Democratic

Party. It would be an innovation for unions as such to participate in politics. Up to then they had always obeyed the dictate laid down by old Samuel Gompers to help their friends and punish their enemies, but to remain independent of political organization. They were chafing at the bit by 1936.

Franklin D. was overlooking no bets in seeking a smashing re-election in 1936, and the labor move was started, under the title of Labor's Non-Partisan League, with Major George Berry of the Pressmen's Union its titular head, and the redoubtable John L. Lewis its financial angel.

Industrial New York was the perfect place for a branch of the league to be set up, and the New York trade-union leaders were called in. They were strong for Roosevelt and his social reforms, they wanted to participate, and they agreed to do so as a legal party, rather than as a labor arm of the Democratic Party, as some advised. Their view was sold to the President by Sidney Hillman, with help from Mrs. Roosevelt and Fiorello H. La Guardia.

The President's chief political lieutenants in New York within the Democratic Party—Jim Farley and Ed Flynn—both had qualms about the step and they protested. They knew it was a good move for the moment, but they worried about the future. The President pooh-poohed their fears, and the Democratic leaders yielded. They helped the new group obtain a place on the ballot for its set of presidential electors, all pledged to Roosevelt, through the complicated petition-getting process required by the election law, described elsewhere in this book. The Democratic Party and the ALP formally nominated a joint slate of presidential electors, consisting of forty-three Democrats and four labor-union leaders identified with the new party. The ALP nominated Herbert H. Lehman for governor, and dutifully took all his Democratic running-mates, generally acting as the tail to the Democratic kite. Roosevelt carried the state by more than a million majority that year. The new party polled 275,000 votes for the joint ticket, a promising start.

These votes came from union members and from old-time Socialists, but they also came from the mothers and grandmothers of union members, old people who had never voted before. They came out of their tenements to vote for the man they had heard on their installment-payment radio sets, for the man who to many of them was the new Messiah. Doctors and lawyers, artists and writers who had never dabbled in politics voted in 1936 and had to produce proof of literacy like all other first voters to do it. Probably most of this new crop voted for Roosevelt on the Democratic line, the first line on the ballot at that time, instead of hunting for the clasped-hands emblem of the ALP, but the latter got its share of the new vote, and this share increased over the years as its voters became more politically sophisticated.

It became obvious in the months immediately following the 1936 election that the American Labor Party was not going to fold up quietly just because its usefulness to the Democrats was temporarily at an end. Its leaders had had a taste of big-time politics; they liked it and they smacked their lips for more.

Their natural next step was to take part in the mayoralty election of 1937 in New York City, where the bulk of the ALP vote had been cast before, and where it has always been cast since then. The natural candidate for the party to support was La Guardia, personally close to the garment-union leaders, mercurial but money-honest, about to run for his second term as reform Mayor.

This was what Farley and Flynn, anxious to regain control of New York City for the Democrats, had feared when in a White House conference they first opposed labor's new venture. And Roosevelt, who always liked the "Little Flower" and thought him useful politically as well as governmentally, may also have had it in mind when he overruled the objections of Flynn and Farley and ordered the party's formation. For, without a vehicle like the ALP, La Guardia would have faced rough going in 1937.

He had been elected in 1933 on the Republican ticket, with aid from a citizenry aroused by Tammany's scandals. Democrats and independents voted for him that year under the emblem of the City Fusion Party, a reform outfit as impermanent as most of its kind. By 1937 the Republicans of the city were tired of La Guardia. They were tired of his political championing of labor and the New Deal, they were tired of his personal rudeness to them, and they did not even have the solace of a good patronage meal in the form of city jobs. The latter were kept scarce for Republicans, and Fiorello made those who were rewarded jump through hoops for their tidbits.

As a result, there was serious discussion, in private conferences, of the Democrats and Republicans getting together on a bipartisan candidate to beat La Guardia. On the surface now this may look like two Goliaths bearing down from different directions on one little David, but little David, or Fiorello, had at that time an unlimited supply of rocks for his slingshot.

The plan to gang up on Fiorello probably would have gone through except for the unquestionably correct conviction held by a few leading Republicans that he would beat the two major parties together, running simply on the American Labor and Fusion tickets. They felt that an outraged populace would have stormed to the polls in presidential-year proportions if confronted with the sight of Tammany and the Republicans lying in the same bed. Tammany had been kicked out of office for corruption only four years before, and the local Republican Party was a professional worshipper at the municipal shrine of clean government.

So the proposed partnership to divide the municipal

spoils collapsed, even though Tammany did back the late Royal S. Copeland, Hearst's United States Senator, in both party primaries, and he lost both. The GOP leaders backed down, gave La Guardia the Republican endorsement, and won political concessions from him in return.

The most important thing to the Labor Party at the time was that it had forced the nomination of La Guardia by the very fact of its existence, and so to all intents and purposes it had elected a Mayor. It did give La Guardia his actual margin of victory. He defeated Jeremiah T. Mahoney by 453,000 votes, and the Labor Party polled 482,790 on its own line.

At that moment of the party's biggest triumph it had just begun to nurture the Communist seeds that sprouted turmoil for years to come. The Labor Party, by polling more than 50,000 votes for its candidate for governor in 1936, had established itself under state law as a legal party, with the right to enroll its membership during registration week and to start having primary elections. The first enrollment for the Labor Party was in 1937 and its first primary in 1938.

I have noted that New York State has a strict primary law. One cannot vote in a party primary unless, during the week set aside for registration for the previous election, he has enrolled in that party. Enrolling carries with it no legal obligation to vote for the party's nominees, but it carries the right to help choose those nominees in the primary and to pick the party officers who are elected in the primary. The set-up was just right for a well-integrated, militant minority like the Communists.

They had lost their official status as a party—descending to the unofficial status of political group—by failing to poll the minimum number of votes for governor in 1936. With the Labor Party in being, they never really tried to regain their official status, usually avoiding the issue by nominating candidates for office other than that of governor, on which the legal recognition depends. They enrolled en masse in the Labor Party instead. They helped organize district clubs, they attended every meeting.

They devoted to the Labor Party that unlimited energy and initiative which has always made Communist influence in political- and economic-minded groups ten times as great as is warranted by the actual membership. In dealing with enrollment and the Communist infiltration into the ALP it should be understood that it was perfectly legal. A Republican may enroll as a Democrat and vice versa. In fact, in the days of Tammany's real power, strong district leaders enrolled enough of their followers in the Republican Party so that if the Republican leader got troublesome he could be unseated in the next primary election in favor of a more complaisant opponent. The Communists did something similar. They kept up their own party as a façade, but each party member was told to enroll in the ALP and vote in the primaries for the Communist-selected candidates for party office.

It was easy for the Communists to take party control in Manhattan, the first county on which they concentrated. To show how it can be worked, the ALP, with an average vote of 400,000, most of it in New York City, usually enrolls about half that number. So 200,000 are entitled to vote in the primary. Possibly twenty-five per cent do vote—and this is a figure true of all parties. In the twenty-five per cent are one hundred per cent of the Communists. Ten thousand Communists would be more than enough to control the party primary in the largest county.

By 1938 it was evident that the Reds had control of the Manhattan organization, though no party split was visible to the public at the time. The old-line garment-union leadership still felt confident that the Communists could not win in Brooklyn or the Bronx, two ALP voting strongholds, nor could they get any strength up-state. The theory proved only partly right.

Up-state, in the counties outside New York City, the cards were stacked against the Communists. The state committee, the governing body of the Labor Party just as it is of the major parties, consisted of five members from each of the 150 Assembly districts in the state. Only 62 of these districts lay, at that time, within the city. Thus on the state committee, five ALP committeemen, recruited with difficulty from the farms of some rural county like Schuyler or Lewis, had a voting strength equal to that of the tremendous Second A.D. of Brooklyn, where the ALP had 17,000 registered and enrolled voters in 1937 and where at times it has actually been the majority party. The Communists had strength in Albany, with fifteen state committee members, but this was more than canceled out by the Rochester garment center with its twenty-five state committeemen.

The first showdown between the left and right wings came in the fall of 1939, when the state committee, anxious to give the public a count of the Communist noses, passed a resolution denouncing the Hitler-Stalin pact, the go-ahead signal for the invasion of Poland. The *Daily Worker*— Communist Party organ—first had refused to believe the news of that pact when it was printed in the "capitalist" newspapers and then began turning rapid somersaults trying to adjust the American Communist party line to the new line from the Kremlin. Just about the time the Reds stopped revolving and had determined their course, the Hillman-Dubinsky-Rose leadership delivered its challenge and the *Daily Worker,* which previously had feigned lack of interest in the ALP, countered with an editorial calling for the reorganization of the party in the interest of peace and democracy.

The Splinter Parties

The lines were thus drawn. To the Old Guard's surprise, the Communists continued to make progress. It was only by a narrow margin in 1940 that the leadership of the party was able to control the state convention—by then the legal nominating body—and endorse Roosevelt for a third term. In 1940 the Communists were against Roosevelt, denouncing him as an imperialist and a warmonger. The party meetings during this period became so acrimonious that managers of hotels and convention halls shied away from renting space to the ALP for meetings, and police riot calls were frequent.

The Communists, who already controlled the party in Manhattan, eventually took over the Brooklyn organization and made gains in Queens. They were slow in getting control of the Bronx, even after the first batch of right-wingers left the party, because in the Bronx the garment-center workers were clustered in packed apartment-house districts and the old-time unionists went to their club meetings early and stayed late. More important, they voted in the primaries every year as long as they stayed in the party.

The rightists fought hard in Brooklyn. They tried to retain control at a raucous county committee meeting, even though the Reds had the votes. One scene there is worth recalling. The leftists had a leader of the New York Newspaper Guild, a mild quiet copyreader, as their candidate for county ALP chairman. The incumbent right-wingers had physical control of the platform at the meeting hall. The leftists boosted their peerless leader, cradled in their arms, toward the rostrum. The right-wingers pressed him downwards with their feet.

There he remained a full two minutes, suspended in mid-air like a human pushball, until his protests convinced his own followers that force was futile. They stopped pushing and went out and got a court injunction. So one by one the Commies took over the county organizations until only the gerrymandered state committee was a sanctuary for the right-wingers, led by Dubinsky and Rose.

Hillman had pulled his union at least halfway out of the party in 1942 by cutting off the payment of dues, and when he took it back, late in 1943, it was under terms that led Dubinsky and Rose, in their turn, to pull out and form the Liberal Party. Hillman and his Amalgamated, Dubinsky and his ILGWU, were respectively the Macy's and Gimbels of the garment unions. Besides constantly competing over union jurisdiction—whose union cut which garments— there were personal differences between Sidney the suave and Dave the direct-actionist. These differences spread to their lieutenants. And there were ideological divergences as well. Hillman had a greater toleration for Communists as long as they stayed out of his union and generally out of his path.

Hillman was by this time a national figure, Dubinsky only a local one. Hillman was labor's representative in the top echelon of the war-production command, working with "big shots" like William Knudsen and Donald Nelson. He was helping to form, and wound up running, the Political Action Committee of the CIO. He was so big that it would have been perfectly logical—though the report has never been authenticated—for President Roosevelt to have said "clear it with Sidney" when the nomination of Harry Truman for vice president in place of Henry Wallace was all decided except for labor approval.

Acting in advance of the 1944 election, Hillman called in Dubinsky and Rose and proposed a unity front for the coming campaign. He wanted all unions in the Labor Party and he was willing to take in the Communists too, with the provision that no Communist should ever be nominated on the ALP ticket for either state or county office. Dubinsky and Rose balked. They wanted an outright ban on the

Commies, which Hillman felt would make the unity move futile. But the Commies accepted the Hillman proposal. There was one more primary fight, with the Hillman unions and the Commies lined up against the Dubinsky crowd. The former won rather easily and the latter marched out to form the Liberal Party.

It was easier for Hillman to make peace with the Communists late in 1943 than it would have been in 1940. They were completely under control in his own union and they were, by then, all out for the war effort, since Hitler had become Stalin's foe as well as America's. They took the lead in keeping strikes in the nation at a minimum, whereas in 1940 they had been inspiring strikes in airplane factories. Hillman kept the Communists under control as long as he lived. He ruled the state committee, while the Commies ran most of the important county organizations. But it was always a delicate alliance. After he died, in 1946, Hyman Blumberg, his right-hand man in the Amalgamated, succeeded to the hot seat.

Into the Liberal Party meanwhile had gone all of Dubinsky's followers. They ran Roosevelt on a separate ticket in 1944, polled enough votes for Jim Mead for governor in 1946—177,418—to become a recognized party, and enrolled their membership in the fall of 1947, becoming thus a fourth full-fledged state-wide party.

While both the American Labor and Liberal parties often have claimed that they furnished the votes to elect the Democratic state and national tickets in 1938, 1940, and 1944—the last the first year the Liberal Party functioned— these claims cannot be accepted at face value. The ALP did average, before the Liberal split-off, about 400,000 votes, and it continued to do so afterward, with the Liberal Party getting 329,235 in 1944. It is true that many thousands of voters were drawn to the polls for the first time by the organizing work of the minor parties, but many thousands of others, probably a majority, would have voted under the Democratic emblem for Roosevelt and such other Democratic standard-bearers as Herbert Lehman if the Labor and Liberal parties had not been on the ballot. To this extent they sapped the strength of the Democrats, while drawing virtually nothing from the Republicans. The 1944 election figures for New York City bear this out.

President Roosevelt carried New York City over Tom Dewey by a 770,000 majority, of which 389,000 came from the Labor Party and 306,000 from the Liberal Party. The actual vote cast on the Democratic line in the traditionally Democratic stronghold of New York City was only 75,000 more than that cast for Dewey on the Republican line. No one would seriously contend that Dewey would have come that close to beating Roosevelt in the five boroughs if the Labor and Liberal parties had not existed.

Roosevelt carried the state as a whole by 316,000, in the face of a vigorous campaign on the part of the Republicans to convince the voters that the Democratic Party was under Communist control because it had accepted the support of the CIO-PAC and the Labor Party. Despite Roosevelt's victories, the effect on the Democratic vote and the Democratic machines was felt seriously in local elections. In Manhattan and Brooklyn in particular, the Democrats dropped from possession of an absolute and foolproof majority over the Republicans to the point where the ALP and Liberal Party votes, or either one of them, was necessary for them to win. Several times, by combining with the ALP or having that group nominate a slate independent of the Democratic ticket, the Republicans won local or judicial offices.

The tie-up of the Communists with the ALP had the effect in 1946—when the ALP was behind the Democratic ticket state-wide, and when the revulsion against Russia's postwar encroachments in Europe first became strong—of driving away from the Democratic candidates many voters who wanted nothing to do with anyone the Communists endorsed, even by indirection. Some county leaders, notably Flynn of the Bronx, began rejecting ALP local endorsements as a liability as early as 1945, and in the winter of 1947 the Democratic state command quietly made up its mind that it would not accept ALP endorsement for the national ticket in 1948 in the state, even if that support could be obtained. The Liberal Party, known to be a right-wing group, posed no such problem and most of the Democrats continued taking Liberal Party endorsements with pleasure.

There was an amusing reversal of tactics engineered on the leftists by the O'Connell organization in Albany. The Communists had early taken control of the ALP there. Later, to their surprise, they found that the O'Connells had enrolled enough surplus Democrats in the ALP in Albany to control the primary and the nominating machinery. The ALP took them to court in 1948 to try to regain control.

Even from the start the alliance between the Democrats and the ALP, whether it was under right- or left-wing control, was not free from friction. The Laborites, in addition to endorsing and electing La Guardia in 1937 and again in 1941, showed their independence of their Democratic state machine, on issues other than support of Roosevelt and Lehman, by declining to endorse two of Lehman's running-mates in the 1938 state election. These two were John J. Bennett, Jr., Attorney General, and Morris S. Tremaine, State Comptroller. Bennett and Tremaine won anyhow, in an otherwise close election, since they were popular in their own party and Republicans up-state voted for them as well, but the seeds of ALP unpopularity in the Democratic organization had been sown.

Again in 1942 it was the insistence of Dubinsky and Rose that they could not get their followers to support Bennett, by then Jim Farley's candidate for governor, that led Roosevelt to withdraw his implied support of Bennett for the nomination and swing to Jim Mead, the move that first openly split the Democratic Party in the state. When Bennett was nominated in spite of this, the Labor Party leaders cast political caution to the winds and named their own state ticket.

Hillman did not approve of the separate ticket, his followers have since said, and they have declared that this was one of the reasons why he temporarily withdrew his financial support from the ALP in 1942. But to Dubinsky and Rose a matter of principle was involved, and it must be said for the garment workers who went into politics that their parties have been governed more by principle and less by considerations of practical politics than the Republicans and the Democrats.

There is an old saying, attributed to various political wits from Jimmy Walker down, that there comes a time in politics when a man—or a party—must rise above principle. The major parties, maintaining extensive organizations by means of job or favor patronage, do not like to contemplate losing an election just for the sake of principle. The effect on the machine is too injurious, too many of its office-holders are dislodged, and if the party through keeping its principles loses too many elections, the completely unprincipled eventually take hold. So they compromise with principle reasonably often.

The major parties exist financially on contributions of persons they have put in office or who have received favors or hope to receive them. Therefore a party too long out of power may run into financial difficulties. This was not true of the splinter parties. The unions belonging to them first paid dues as unions, so much per member; and after this was barred by law, their members paid as individuals. In addition, collections are frequently taken at conventions or county committee meetings, something that would never be attempted at a Republican or Democratic conclave.

The original ALP and its successor, the Communist Party, and the Liberal Party all can lose election after election and still hold their followers. Patronage to them is welcome, but unessential. They can afford to fight for social programs that in the longer run they hope will benefit their members. Thus, the ALP and the Liberal Party during the Roosevelt era never deviated from Roosevelt's social program, and if they could not find an available major-party candidate pledged to those aims, they nominated one of their own without worrying over the fact that he was a sure loser.

This was not true of candidates for local office. There practical political aims often overshadowed governing principles. While the natural alliance of the ALP and the Liberal party was with the Democrats, there was many a deviation in favor of the Republicans, for local considerations.

The splinter groups, in their rivalry, sometimes made endorsements of major-party candidates depend on which major party accepted the endorsement of the other minor party. In 1945, for example, when it became evident that the Democrats would nominate William O'Dwyer for mayor and that he would have the support of the ALP, the Liberal Party felt it had to ally itself with the Republicans to maintain its political position. It made a particularly bad deal in this case, for while the Republicans accepted Jonah J. Goldstein, the Tammany Democrat who was the Liberal Party's choice for a mayoralty nominee, Goldstein made a miserable race, and both parties regretted the alliance even before election day. The selection of Goldstein was designed to consolidate Jewish voters into the Liberal Party and was accepted by Governor Dewey in order to remove from the mouths of Jewish voters a bad taste left by some aspects of the presidential campaign of 1944. But, as noted before, the Jews have voted solidly only for men of the Lehman caliber, and Goldstein did not quite fill the bill.

By 1947 the Republicans and Democrats alike were tired of bargaining over dual nominations with the minor parties and they also were interested in preventing minor parties from raiding their primaries and walking out with major-party nominations. So they joined in passing the Wilson-Pakula law, which provided that a man who is not a member of a party could enter its primary only with the permission of the party organization, as represented by the county committee of the area involved.

The law was one of the first heavy blows struck at the splinter parties in the postwar era. The second was the repeal of proportional representation that same year, a step which seemed likely to deprive the minor groups of representation in the City Council, their soap-box inside City Hall.

The next major blow to the ALP's balance-wheel position—and it was a matter of deliberate choice on the part of the Communist leadership—came with the announcement of Henry A. Wallace, at the start of 1948, that he would be a candidate for president on a third-party ticket. The ALP became the principal organized force behind him in New York State, and the Amalgamated Clothing Workers, the old Hillman crowd, pulled out of the party as soon as Wallace declared his intentions. The differences between the Amalgamated and the International Ladies Garment Workers Union, headed by Dubinsky, were too great to permit the Amalgamated to go into the Liberal Party, and it contented itself, for the time being, with such political action as was sponsored by the American Federation of Labor on a national scale.

The Amalgamated's withdrawal left the Communists in full and undisputed control of the Labor Party, with the election advantages that the latter's more respectable name gave the Reds on the ballot. Those associated with the party claimed that there would be, as the years went on, an increasing "polarization" of the vote, that is, more votes cast on the extreme right and extreme left of the political spectrum, and fewer in the middle positions occupied by the Democrats under Roosevelt, and the old American Labor and Liberal parties. This is the extreme division the Communists have always sought.

Chapter VIII

THE MACHINES

The last time an election was stolen in New York City
was in 1933, when Tammany, fighting a losing battle to
save its power and prestige, elected a Borough President
and a District Attorney by a margin of about 12,000 votes,
all fraudulent. Those were the only offices it managed to
salvage that year out of the anti-machine landslide that
elected Fiorello La Guardia as Mayor for the first time. In
the long run Tammany, known nation-wide as the prototype of machine politics, would have been better off if it
had not stolen the prosecutor's office. Its District Attorney
was picked by men interested in protecting rather than
prosecuting the underworld, and the state-sponsored Dewey
investigation two years later was the inevitable result.

The theft of an election, like that of 1933, probably won't
happen again, or not for a long time. Tammany was desper-
ate, but still strong, because it had the racket mobs and the
police department was under its control. Squads of mobster
"storm troopers," trade-marked for their own purposes by
identical pearl-gray fedoras, marched in on polling place
after polling place south of Fourteenth Street in Manhattan
and took over the voting machinery.

They told the policeman assigned to the place to "beat
it," and he, knowing where the interest of his superiors lay,
took a walk around the block instead of sounding a riot
call. The citizenry, waiting in line to vote, was shoved out
of the way. One gorilla—one who was able to write—would

take over the registry book and sign for those who had not
yet voted, while another rang up the votes on the voting
machine, as if it were a cash register. From start to finish
it was just a show of force and, because of that, was limited
in its application to the sections of the county where lived
the poorer and less educated voters—where such tactics had
the most chance of success without interference.

Interference was tried. Fiorello La Guardia's campaign
manager, William M. Chadbourne, raised his bull-like voice
in protest, but was arrested for disorderly conduct and
marched off to the hoosegow. Things really were rough
that day.

But all this was the adrenalin-inspired struggle of a dying
political machine, the Tammany Hall whose name had
been synonomous with power and corruption in municipal
politics. And even for the limited success it achieved, it
needed the connivance of a police department whose members had grown used to the system, the theory of political
action that permitted the underworld to get away with
murder.

It would take many years of municipal decay—and the
trend is not noticeably that way—to bring back the 1933
conditions to New York City. Now the police are held personally responsible for conditions in polling places; the
entire machinery of the city, state, and national governments is geared to prevent election frauds. The check on
possible major-party collusion has been greater because of
the existence of the organized minor parties, entitled to
polls watchers and capable of manning each booth with
experienced people.

Tammany could never have stolen enough votes, even
under 1933 conditions, to carry the mayoralty election that
year. Tammany and similar machines in the other counties
had not depended on stolen votes to win elections in New
York for many years. Excepting the time at the turn of the

century when ballot-boxes containing votes for Wil Randolph Hearst for mayor were found floating in East River the day after election, the machines did no steal on a scale large enough to affect a city-wide election. Men in a position to know definitely estimate that since the days of voting machines there never have been cast more than 40,000 fraudulent votes in a city-wide election, and of these probably 30,000 were cast in Manhattan.

That is a puny percentage of the total vote, compared, for example, with Kansas City, where 80,000 fraudulent names were taken off the election rolls—so much smaller to begin with—as the result of one investigation. Moreover it is a fair guess that from 1938 on, when automatic re-counts were ordered by the Legislature, not as many as 10,000 illegal votes have been cast in the metropolis in any one election. In state-wide elections these Democratic city thefts are at least counterbalanced by that many illegitimate votes up-state, where the Republicans would be in equivalent position to commit the larceny.

It is still possible to steal a primary election, where paper ballots are used and where the public interest is not focused on the result. But in a general election, not only has it become impossible, but the will to do it no longer exists. There are few these days in any political organization, the Communists excepted, who are willing to go to jail, or risk going, for a political cause.

The Scottoriggio case, in which a Republican election district captain was fatally beaten while on his way to the polls to insist on a fair count in the election of 1946, was an exception that proved the rule. It occurred in East Harlem, the last stronghold in New York of an old-time political machine. The machine flourished in the only section of the city where a newly arrived population, in this case Puerto Rican, was dominant and furnished good machine material.

The Machines

Immigration built the political machines in New York City, starting 'way back with the flood of the Irish, and the machines were struck a death blow when the nation embarked, after World War I, on a policy of restricted immigration through the quota system. The machines did not show the effects until much later, but the cutting off of large-scale immigration deprived them of most of their annual crop of prospective voters, people whom they could help become citizens, people in a strange country, having to learn a new language. These people needed the helping hand extended by Tammany and its allies and were in return willing, even eager, to hand over their family bloc of votes. The second generation in those families, born here, better educated, better off financially, usually grew away from the dependence their parents had had on the district leader and his leg-man, the election district or precinct captain. But up to the cutting off of immigration, there was always a new group of arrivals to be taken into the fold.

The second most important factor in the decline of the machines was the social-welfare program put into effect under the New Deal. It is a political paradox that the machines all over the country turned in their greatest majorities for and under Franklin D. Roosevelt, implementing the social program that was cutting their own throats.

In the old days—in fact, up to 1931—it was against the law in New York State for public funds to be used for the support of anyone outside a public institution. To be fed or housed, you had to go to the poorhouse as far as any agency of government was concerned. This meant that the man who was temporarily down and out got his aid from his local political machine. The leader had a ready two bucks in his pocket—in days when two bucks meant something—and his card, with a scribbled notation, was always good for a job shoveling snow for the city or digging a ditch for the gas company. The Christmas and Thanksgiving baskets meant holiday cheer for those who otherwise would not have had the means to celebrate; the annual outing of the Umteenth Ward Democratic Club meant a neighborhood picnic for those in whose lives picnics were rare.

The Roosevelt program produced home relief and unemployment relief, which kept families together; it brought aid to widows and dependent children—aid they got as a matter of right from government and not as a favor from a political machine. It is true that the people on WPA and home relief voted for Roosevelt en masse in the 1936 election, but in New York at least, they did it as a matter of economics, or in gratitude, not as the result of compulsion.

Which leads to the basic and fundamental fact about the political machines of today. It is that even when a machine wins and wins overwhelmingly, it does so without actually controlling the vote cast.

The people vote for machine candidates when they want to, not because they have to. There is no personal obligation to the machine for money, food, or jobs. The old intimate contact between ward captain and voter does not exist. It was a long time before political observers noted this trend. It was well hidden because during the period when the decay was eating at the vitals of the machines, they happened to have, in New York City and state, a remarkable series of vote-getting candidates at the top of their tickets who attracted the electorate.

In New York City there is an apparently irreducible minimum of about 700,000 voters who will vote for anyone on the Democratic ticket, and slightly more than 300,000 who will vote for anyone on the Republican ticket. These are bed-rock figures and fall short, by hundreds of thousands of votes, of being enough to elect a candidate to major office. But to the Democratic minimums Smith, Jimmy Walker, Roosevelt, and Lehman added so much strength in their own right that the machine leaders could point with pride to the enormous majorities their organizations rolled up in the machine counties. Some even kidded themselves into thinking they and their boys were responsible.

Two anecdotes of personal experience show otherwise. I lived for five years in the home bailiwick of the late John H. McCooey, undisputed leader of the powerful Democratic organization in Brooklyn. The district was one that turned in, each year, tremendous "machine" majorities. There were four votes in the family, the owners of a two-story house. Not once in those five years, in a presidential, gubernatorial, or local election, did a Democratic captain ring the doorbell to ask the family to register or to influence its possible voting tendencies. And this was nearly twenty years ago. Again, in 1945, a mayoralty election year, I lived for a short period on Manhattan's West Side, in Chelsea. It is so traditionally a Democratic machine area that today seven district leaders are still crammed politically into a space only big enough for one, each striving to keep up the appearance of power long since gone, along with the population that was its source. And in that area, where doorbell-ringing at election time was as matter-of-course in the old days as holly wreaths in store windows at Christmas, no Democratic party worker ever appeared. The only campaign literature received was slipped under the door by the Communist Party. The traditional machines no longer even try to deliver or influence the vote.

With that in mind, a description of the important political machines of both major parties in the city and state follows:

NEW YORK COUNTY

The basic trouble with Tammany is that the present members still look back to the days when it was the dom-

inant organization in the city. They have tried to keep the
machine geared to the old ratio of power and patronage, to
maintain that higher standard of political living which was
theirs when they ran the city, and no longer can be kept up
on the purse of a single county organization.

Tammany had so much, in the old days, that it suffered
far more than any of the other county organizations when
it lost control of City Hall in 1933, with the election of
La Guardia. The others had lived off their county patronage, plus the bits Tammany let them have from the city
trough. It is probable that Tammany could have survived
one or two terms of La Guardia as Mayor, still possessing,
as it did for a while, control of the magistrates' courts and
the county offices. But before La Guardia was through,
county offices and county government had been wiped out,
or placed on a civil-service merit basis. And magistrates
serve only ten-year terms.

By the time the Little Flower left City Hall, at the end
of twelve years of independent, anti-machine rule, there
was not—there could not be—a single person outside of the
state and county courts who owed his job and therefore his
primary allegiance to Tammany rather than to La Guardia.

The organization went bankrupt in more ways than one.
Its new Wigwam on Seventeenth street, built to order in
prosperous days, was sold out from under it by the bank
that held the mortgage. The International Ladies Garment
Workers Union, the "pantspressers in politics," took it over
as headquarters. Tammany was reduced to a political scav-
enger status. Judgeship-selling became more prevalent.
There were reports that even appointments as secretaries
and court attendants had "for sale" tags on them. Still later
the ruling clique in the Hall was reduced to the ignominy
of the alliance with Marcantonio referred to elsewhere.
Tammany, which once had run the city, had to get its favors
and its protection second-hand.

The Machines

It would be pleasant to report that Tammany had shown some signs of either reforming, or recovering its leadership since 1933. Curry, the very fine district leader whose obstinacy made him the worst county leader, went out in 1934, to be followed by a whole series of leaders who did not fill the bill. Jim Dooling had the capacity, but was ill, and a sick man can not function in a job that requires sometimes the tact of an ambassador and at others the brass of a burglar. Christie Sullivan was slow mentally. Mike Kennedy lacked background. Ed Loughlin was just a "front."

Through all those years and county leaderships Tammany's individual district leaders seemed to show little sign of understanding that times had changed. The caliber of their candidates for office was not improved. I recall checking one election eve in a La Guardia campaign with one of the most important and quickest-witted members of the Hall. What did he think was going to happen in the mayoralty race to be settled the next day?

"I think the best man will win," said the political light, and both he and I knew exactly whom he meant.

Years later, when O'Dwyer came in as Democratic Mayor, one of his first acts was to demand a "reform" in the Hall, a cleaning up. Loughlin was thrown out, as were Clarence H. Neal and Bert Stand, the brains behind Loughlin. The alliance with Marcantonio was broken off. All this was done by the district leaders, unwillingly in most cases, but knowing that they had to change the scenery to get any of the O'Dwyer patronage they needed so badly.

Frank J. Sampson, a pleasant man, new as a district leader, became county leader at O'Dwyer's behest. He rides uneasy herd on two different blocs, the "Irish" and the "Italians," with his own real support coming from the Irish leaders, who do not form a majority of the committee. One may credit Mr. Sampson with the best of intentions, but it

is doubtful if he can crack down too hard on the remnants of the pirate crew.

As a factor in New York County, Tammany has its importance. It has maintained its old-time substantial lead in enrollment, as the figures for the last presidential, mayoralty, and gubernatorial election years show:

ELECTION	DEMOCRATIC	REPUBLICAN	ALP
1944	450,577	193,354	41,395
1945	308,837	93,388	49,499
1946	338,042	181,613	57,751

The election results are often different, however. In New York County, as elsewhere, enrolled Democrats have been inclined to vote under the American Labor or Liberal party emblems, pulling the Democratic vote consistently under the party's enrollment. The figures for the same three elections follow:

ELECTION	DEMOCRATIC	REPUBLICAN	ALP	LIBERAL
1944	350,750	258,516	96,511	62,559
1945 *	189,917	76,802	63,554	21,617
1946	212,718	264,990	80,995	32,175

* The 1945 mayoralty election was the only one of the three in which the Democratic, American Labor, and Liberal party votes were not cast for the same head of the ticket. In that year, it must be remembered, O'Dwyer received the Democratic and ALP nominations, Goldstein the Republican and Liberal; and Newbold Morris ran independently, getting more than 400,000 votes in the city at large.

In weighing Tammany's position, one must remember that the votes it once controlled are no longer there, even if Tammany could control them. Manhattan, for twenty years, has been in the process of being transformed into a business and management terminal, with no room for low-rent slums. A single improvement like the Holland Tunnel wiped out six blocks of tenements for its plaza, and the voters never came back. Once the largest of the five boroughs and now second to Brooklyn, it probably will slip

128

into fourth place in the next decade, below the Bronx and Queens. With the loss of people, it has also lost congressional and legislative representation and the prestige that goes with large blocs of votes. If Tammany ever regains the ascendancy in the city and state that it had in the days of Charles F. Murphy, it will be as the result of many years of careful rebuilding of political fences. Such a program is not clearly in sight.

Among New York County's Republicans, the organization trend is upward rather than down, but the GOP still has a long way to go to attain any rank. The party's plight goes back to the days of Sam Koenig, ousted as leader in 1933. In most of the twenty-two years that Koenig tried to keep his machine operating, his party's stands on state and national issues were contrary to the thinking of the majority of the people, and therefore he couldn't win an election. Koenig was a man of character and integrity, but his district leaders lived all during national prohibition on the pickings they got from dry-law corruption, plus a little federal patronage. Koenig took the rap, in the public's mind, and in the political ferment of 1933 the "old man" was beaten in a primary fight.

After an interim Kenneth F. Simpson took over, in 1935, and under his ebullient leadership the party perked up considerably, but it never had much patronage to grease its wheels until Tom Dewey became Governor and his personal lieutenant, Tom Curran, became county chairman. Its lack of a definite hold on the voters is best illustrated by the figures for the 1945 mayoralty election. Goldstein, the mayoralty nominee picked by Curran, Dewey, and the Liberal Party, got 76,802 votes on the Republican ticket, while Newbold Morris, La Guardia's candidate, received 100,064 votes in the county, nearly all of them from Republicans.

But the New York County Republicans have received a very substantial share of state patronage, and, on a county-wide basis, by dealing with the ALP or the Democrats, they have been able occasionally to elect a judge or a county officeholder. Formerly its ability to get a candidate into office had been limited to the confines of the silk-stocking congressional and senatorial district dominated by upper Fifth, Madison, and Park avenues. The Republican organization is more alive and alert than it was, but if the GOP should lose the Governorship and not get any federal patronage, its position would not be good.

BROOKLYN

Back in the last century, the Democratic boss of Coney Island, John Y. McKane, stole enough votes for his party's ticket to swing the state and the presidential election to Grover Cleveland. Apart from that, the Brooklyn Democratic crowd has always operated on a reasonably conservative basis. In the early part of the current century Brooklyn went Republican as often as not, but as the tomato fields and potato patches gave way to two-family dwellings, inhabited by refugees from Manhattan's crowded streets, the borough became more and more Democratic in its voting tendencies. In 1927 the organization, then headed by John H. McCooey, scored its first clean sweep, electing every alderman, assemblyman, and county officeholder.

McCooey was a fat, ruddy-faced little man who could have posed without make-up as Santa Claus in any Fulton Street department store. And he was Santa Claus to the Kings County Democrats, bringing them to the top of the world politically. Smith and Roosevelt helped with their vote-getting power, of course.

There is the story of the candidate for a minor judgeship, who was expected to win easily in Roosevelt's first campaign for the Presidency. But he developed an acute case of candidatitis—he hadn't seen his name mentioned in the papers and he was sure he was going to be licked. He stood in McCooey's receiving line one Monday morning, intending to unburden himself on the county boss. But his local district leader saw him first, knew what was on his mind, and yanked him by the ear over to a corner.

The leader said: "Look. You've seen a ferryboat pull into a slip. When it pulls in, it pulls a lot of garbage in with it. Stop worrying. Roosevelt is a ferryboat."

McCooey, in his dotage, hooked up too closely with Curry's leadership of Tammany Hall, and the two managed to drag their organizations down into friendless defeat. "Uncle John" died a year later, in 1934, and he was succeeded by an even defter man, Frank V. Kelly, who took an organization that had been hit hard, that was ready for strife and dissension, and he kept it toeing the mark for another dozen years. Kelly was independent financially, with a substantial income from an insurance business. He kept the machine clean and he consistently followed the policies of Roosevelt and Lehman, which was all he really needed to do. He never could defeat La Guardia in the county, but neither was anyone else successful in doing so in New Deal territory when La Guardia had the Roosevelt blessing.

The enrollment figures for the borough are impressive for the Democrats:

ELECTION	DEMOCRATIC	REPUBLICAN	ALP
1944	715,904	256,158	83,244
1945	513,468	105,120	89,782
1946	563,915	207,902	102,961

The election figures for the same years:

ELECTION	DEMOCRATIC	REPUBLICAN	ALP	LIBERAL
1944	475,866	396,866	155,544	132,195
1945 *	293,515	104,750	92,816	53,452
1946	311,516	353,846	140,817	67,890

* Morris received 136,632 votes for mayor.

It is interesting to note that Democratic party strength was so low everywhere in 1946 that even in Brooklyn it took the margins furnished by the American Labor and Liberal parties to give Mead, the party's gubernatorial nominee, a majority in the county. This compares with the 366,739 majority Roosevelt received in 1944, roughly 50,000 more than his total margin in the state.

Kelly died before the 1946 election, and John Cashmore, the Borough President, was elected leader. The influence of Mayor O'Dwyer—who declared for Cashmore while the district leaders were still debating the choice—and that of members of the judiciary who had been Kelly's closest advisers, put him in. Tradition of long standing was broken when Cashmore was picked, since he was a Protestant coming after an unbroken line of Irish-Catholic leaders.

Cashmore, affable, and with a good record in government, remained faced, after he assumed the leadership, with substantial opposition within his party. It came from a group, headed by Kenneth F. Sutherland, that might have prevented his election if Mayor O'Dwyer had not intervened in Cashmore's behalf.

Despite this, and the possibility of trouble ahead, the Brooklyn organization has continued to look good when compared with Tammany. It has behind it the largest bloc of voters of Democratic tendencies anywhere in the East. It has put a succession of reasonably good men into public office and has given the public little to complain about, except for a brief period when the county prosecutor's office was in poor hands and racketeers ran wild.

In the opposite corner has been a Brooklyn Republican organization that never amounted to much. For years its leaders were only figureheads, with little to give in the way of patronage or to contribute to party policies. In 1934 the last of these figureheads, Frederick J. H. Kracke, whose chief claim to fame was that for more than forty years he had never been off the payroll of some public treasury—a feat remarkable for anyone and particularly notable for a Republican—gave up the job to keep a payroll post under La Guardia. John R. Crews, a former pugilist, assumed the leadership and retains it at this writing. Crews turned out to be a much better than average practical politician. He is a plugger. With the help of state patronage from the Dewey administration, to which he has always been loyal, he has put the organization in better condition than ever before.

But the party in Brooklyn has no real solid foundation, and it seems destined to remain in a minority for years to come.

THE BRONX

The best political machine in the city has been run since 1922 by Edward J. Flynn, the polished and urbane lawyer who is the Bronx County Democratic chairman and Democratic national committeeman from New York, and who was Democratic national chairman as well during the 1940 campaign, when Jim Farley dropped the reins in the third-term Roosevelt race. Flynn's national status was ruined by the "paving-block scandal" mentioned earlier. President Roosevelt withdrew his nomination as minister to Australia at Flynn's request because of the hubbub, but no one has ever successfully questioned his leadership of the Bronx Democrats.

Flynn's leadership is unique in that he runs the organization the way a good business executive, risen through the ranks, would direct a large corporation. He set up a smooth-working system, picked trustworthy deputies, and has not bothered himself with details. He is not the boss who sits patiently at the head of a receiving line in county headquarters every Monday to pass personally on hundreds of requests. He is seldom there, nor is he continually being consulted by his lieutenants at his prosperous midtown Manhattan law office.

Flynn and Franklin D. Roosevelt were close friends, socially as well as politically. They swapped yarns and talked politics as equals around the fireplace in the Roosevelt home or in the White House, highball in hand. Flynn benefited in state and national prestige from this association— an association he had earned by his loyalty and his daring in one of three major political gambles Flynn took in the course of his career.

The first of these gambles was when in the pre-Roosevelt days he supported Al Smith in Smith's successful effort to get rid of John F. Hylan as Mayor. Walker, who succeeded Hylan, thereafter recognized Flynn as a leader in his own right, instead of as merely a vassal of Tammany Hall, which had ruled the Bronx directly when the Bronx was a part of New York County.

The second gamble directly concerned Roosevelt. Flynn had been named Secretary of State by Roosevelt in New York State when Roosevelt was Governor. Roosevelt made the move so that he would not have to reappoint to the post Robert Moses, then closely associated with Smith. Flynn had obligations to Smith, however, and when it became evident that Roosevelt was gunning for the Presidency, Flynn went to Smith and asked him if Smith himself, defeated in 1928, was going to seek the nomination again in 1932. Smith assured him he would not, he was through. Flynn plumped for Roosevelt, and stuck with him even after Smith changed his mind and became a candidate for the nomination. Bronx organization sentiment was for Smith, but Flynn stood by his guns. He never suffered for having done so.

His third gamble came when, knowing that the Democratic city ticket picked by Tammany in 1933 was destined to get a terrific shellacking, he put into the race a third city-wide ticket headed by Joseph V. McKee. The McKee ticket finished second to La Guardia's and its presence in the contest saved Flynn from losing his county offices. All three gambles required imagination and courage.

In addition, Flynn had the background and personal tolerance to keep peace in an organization run by the Irish, but dependent largely on the Jewish and Italian overflow from Manhattan for its votes. He built up local confidence in himself and his nominees by close scrutiny of prosecuting officers and the judiciary in his county. Justice could not be bought or sold there, and the public came to know it. Flynn himself recalls that a noted racketeer who lived in Westchester County and had business offices in Manhattan could get home daily only by crossing the Hudson River via the Holland Tunnel to New Jersey and recrossing it via the Bear Mountain Bridge many miles to the north. Had he entered the Bronx, he would have been clapped into the hoosegow.

The registration and election figures for the Bronx tell part of the story. The registration figures:

YEAR	DEMOCRATIC	REPUBLICAN	ALP
1944	408,959	121,794	55,700
1945	300,794	50,573	65,035
1946	331,655	106,603	71,750

The vote:

YEAR	DEMOCRATIC	REPUBLICAN	ALP	LIBERAL
1944	265,591	211,158	98,926	86,008
1945 *	161,499	56,812	66,321	36,612
1946	181,904	192,459	99,632	48,492

* The Morris vote for mayor was 88,464.

Despite the 1946 vote, the Bronx Republican organization is a decrepit group, really no menace at all to the

Democrats. Flynn's Republican vis-à-vis, John J. Knewitz, holds an appointive public job under Democratic judges, which has led to the charge that, politically speaking, he is on Flynn's payroll. Real live opposition has been given by the ALP, which was the second party in the county in the 1945 election, and defeated the Flynn organization in a congressional by-election in 1948. The latter first demonstrated the weakness of Harry S. Truman as a candidate, since his prestige was involved. It showed also that the Flynn organization was, like all the others, suffering from decay, and would probably fall apart whenever Mr. Flynn quit the leadership.

SUBURBIA

Just as the Democratic machines dominate New York City, their Republican counterparts run the suburbs, Westchester on the north and Nassau, with more rural Suffolk, occupying all of Long Island east of the city line.

For purposes of political computation, the suburban counties have always been lumped as "up-state," along with the 54 other counties outside New York City proper. But there is a vast difference between the Westchester and Nassau population and politics and the rest of the up-state territory.

Governmentally Westchester and Nassau operate under county charters that are new and distinctive; politically they represent a constantly increasing percentage of the voting power of the state while the balance of "up-state" decreases in importance. The two counties have grown tremendously in population every decade, and the current one will probably show the greatest growth of all. The additional population comes largely from New York City, where there is no room for people who want trees and grass or a

The Machines

back yard in which Junior may romp. Most of the migrants have been Democrats, and this may affect the voting trends in the next few years, since persons of more modest incomes have been driven out of New York City by the housing shortage there. But up to the present the conservatism that attaches itself usually to suburban living has dominated the politics of these counties.

In Westchester the figures are:

	ENROLLMENT		
YEAR	DEMOCRATIC	REPUBLICAN	ALP
1944	67,617	170,418	2,340
1946	45,887	160,836	3,220

	THE VOTE			
YEAR	DEMOCRATIC	REPUBLICAN	ALP	LIBERAL
1944	91,461	174,635	10,353	5,778
1946	48,826	173,225	7,667	2,755

In Nassau the comparable figures are:

	ENROLLMENT		
YEAR	DEMOCRATIC	REPUBLICAN	ALP
1944	44,171	164,656	1,384
1946	28,284	150,119	1,530

	THE VOTE			
YEAR	DEMOCRATIC	REPUBLICAN	ALP	LIBERAL
1944	68,137	159,713	5,616	4,759
1946	33,812	152,650	4,840	1,995

Westchester and Nassau contain whole cities plus villages within the old established town lines, all grown together or growing together. Attempts to run them with separate governments along traditional lines collapsed a decade ago. A new system was put in, combining city and county government features. A county executive rules the county just as does the mayor of a city, and the County Board of Supervisors serves as the governing body under him. The plan has served to integrate governmental functions as well as political rule.

In Nassau the county boss, J. Russel Sprague, became county executive as soon as the job was created. Sprague is of the newer generation of leaders, smooth, efficient, unostentatious. He succeeded Kenneth F. Simpson as national committeeman from the state, and for years was closest of all the county leaders to Thomas E. Dewey. The mutual endearment lessened a trifle, and in the spring of 1948 Sprague was hoping eventually to retire and spend his time to better advantage on his deep-sea fishing boat. The Nassau machine he ran was always a tight one, with no revolt ever seriously threatened. It was a particularly neat combination of city machine and county organization, smart enough to keep the people happy and bury its own dead.

Westchester, to the north, once was run by William L. Ward, a prosperous manufacturer and close-mouthed boss, willing to help run the state organization or fight it as he chose. In the early thirties, when the Legislature was attempting the probe of New York City that was to become known as the Seabury investigation, Ward blocked the move for months by ordering his Westchester legislative contingent to oppose it. It took a call from the White House, from Herbert Hoover in person, to get Ward to release his people. Whatever Ward's reasons were for opposing the investigation, no one ever questioned his authority. Things are different in the county now.

While the party majorities have continued to grow, no one figure has ever emerged as the complete boss since Ward's death. William F. Bleakley, the party's candidate for governor in 1936, came close, but has gradually given up participation in the leadership. Jane H. Todd, vice-chairman of the state committee, has also been a force, with Herbert C. Gerlach, the county executive, and Livingston Platt, the county chairman, sharing most of the control.

There is a boss in Suffolk, the third of the suburban counties, in the person of W. Kingsland Macy, the former state chairman who battled the public-utility control of the Republican Party years ago. Macy, famous for his starched wing collars as well, is now a Representative in Congress, yearning for the United States Senatorship.

But he never let his personal ambitions interfere with the party welfare, and the majorities he turned in for the ticket were impressive. In 1944 Suffolk added about 34,000 majority to the 168,000 majority Dewey had over Roosevelt in Nassau and Westchester; in 1946 it added 46,000 to Dewey's majority of 235,000 in the other two counties. Nowhere in suburbia is there a Democratic organization capable of challenging the Republicans, outside of individual cities like Yonkers in Westchester and Long Beach in Nassau, two Democratic islands of poor governmental repute.

UP-STATE CITIES

The O'Connell machine in Albany is probably closest to the ideal of the practical politician. It more nearly resembles the old-type Tammany organization, of Murphy's day, than any other extant. It is a prototype of the Irish-Democratic organizations so familiar in the cities of the north, but is much better than most now in existence. It has the vices of entrenched paternalism and plenty of the practical virtues as well. But, good or bad, the people of Albany like it, and the machine has been able to beat off direct attacks on it by the Dewey administration. So strongly was it entrenched that Dewey, directing the warfare from the State Capitol across the park from the O'Connell City Hall, finally gave up. Even the infiltration of Republican officeholders, brought to Albany by GOP state patronage, has not been able to reduce the O'Connell machine majorities.

At one point in the Dewey battle to break the O'Connells, the Governor ordered the seizure of the city records, and state accountants took physical possession of City Hall, on the pretext that a "shortage" existed in the Albany city accounts. The shortage did not exist, and the hope of the Governor's office that some evidence of other scandal could be uncovered while the Governor's men were on the job never materialized.

The O'Connell organization has been accused of most of the high political crimes, and it has been guilty of some of them, like high-pressuring the sale of the product of the family-owned brewery, or finagling with real-estate assessments, lowering them for friends and raising them for foes. The organization has also made some money from poolrooms and from other privileges more legitimately licensed by the city. Tapped telephone conversations have revealed that it would even try to influence a judge in a political case before him.

But, on the plus side, it cleaned up organized vice in Albany at the request of Al Smith when he was Governor. It has never sold a political job, has kept promotion in the organization on a merit basis, and lastly and most important it has given Albany a succession of good local administrations. John Boyd Thacher and Erastus Corning, 2nd, the last two Mayors, were excellent representatives of the old Dutch families still important in the city's life. City services are better than average and not too expensive.

The O'Connell ability to deliver the vote is phenomenal. In 1936, when Roosevelt was at the height of his drawing power, the Albany machine gave him a majority of 18,000. Four years later, with Willkie buttons to be seen all over Albany's main streets, and a major revolt apparently in progress, the Roosevelt majority in the county was still 18,000.

In the last two elections, when the Dewey power was at its greatest, the Albany situation was as follows:

	ENROLLMENT		
YEAR	DEMOCRATIC	REPUBLICAN	ALP
1944	37,373	10,821	241
1946	45,532	10,157	526

	THE VOTE		
YEAR	DEMOCRATIC	REPUBLICAN	ALP	LIBERAL
1944	43,784	30,887	3,106	399
1946	43,646	29,370	4,263	914

In mayoralty elections the Republican opposition to the O'Connell organization falls off to nothing at all, and a Democratic landslide of 40,000 has occurred once or twice.

The O'Connell organization has been kept going partly on the basis of personal loyalty to the family. The head of the clan at this writing is Dan, brother of the founder, Ed, who died half a dozen years ago. And there is no better example of its smart leadership than in its dealings with the American Labor Party, which in Albany was under left-wing control for years. Finally the O'Connells got bored with the trouble the Reds caused, and enrolled enough of their own henchmen as American Labor Party members to take over party control in the primaries. There is not another Democratic organization in the state with the disciplined membership to accomplish that feat.

Nor would another leadership spare that many faithful adherents from its own party ranks, for fear it might need them to quash a primary revolt at some time. There are no primary fights in Albany in the Democratic ranks, and just for an additional margin of safety the Albany machine runs satellite organizations in Green Island and Cohoes, which balance GOP majorities in the rest of the county and leave the Albany city margin the majority in the county as well.

The Albany County Republican organization is unimportant. It lived for years on crumbs given it by the O'Connells, plus hopes for a bigger share. It has fared well under the Dewey state administration and the county chairman, Kenneth S. MacAffer, has prospered in his dual role as local patronage-dispenser and lobbyist for important interests before the Legislature.

Syracuse, one hundred and fifty miles west of Albany on the barge-canal route, is another city where politics and whisky are taken straight—only it is the Republicans who are in control. A decade ago there was an Assemblyman, Horace Stone, who was a thorn in the side of that party. He was also the law partner of the Mayor and county chairman, rough-and-tumble "Rolly" Marvin. Marvin persuaded Stone to run for the state Senate, a somewhat tougher race, and then his own party organization proceeded to give Stone the works and retire him from politics.

Years later Marvin, out as Mayor and trying for a comeback, ran for the state Senate himself and was slaughtered by his own party, ending Marvin's long period as political boss. Marvin had made the error of backing Wendell L. Willkie against Tom Dewey for president in 1940 and compounded it by sticking to Willkie during the years that followed. Dewey set up an opposing state patronage-dispenser in the city and soon lifted Marvin's political scalp.

Party control passed then into the hands of a group of lawyers—Syracuse law firms have been famous in the state—whose members have always furnished advice and money-raising talents for the party. They may compete for legal business, but they unite when their party is in danger. Charles A. McNett is titular county chairman.

Organized labor, though strong in the railroads of which Syracuse is a center, has not been able to cut down too much the old-time Republican majorities in Onondaga County, which includes Syracuse, because there is a big rural vote outside the city.

As noted elsewhere, it is a manifestation of a good Democratic year when that party carries the cities in the industrial belt west of Albany. It takes an exceptional year, however, for the Democrats to carry the counties in which those cities are located. Roosevelt carried Syracuse by 2,000 in 1944, but lost the county by some 7,000, net. The figures for Onondaga County are:

	ENROLLMENT		
YEAR	DEMOCRATIC	REPUBLICAN	ALP
1944	35,068	100,096	840
1946	22,929	94,043	918

	THE VOTE			
YEAR	DEMOCRATIC	REPUBLICAN	ALP	LIBERAL
1944	64,729	80,507	7,922	911
1946	37,204	82,641	3,575	560

The Democratic organization in Onondaga County is about on a par with the Republican organization in the Bronx.

Still farther west is Rochester, one of the busiest, most attractive cities of its size in the nation. Politically, it is the product of a well-established big-business paternalism.

The late George Eastman, Kodak magnate, took over the running of the city more than three decades ago, when it was news for a big businessman to interest himself actively in civic affairs. Eastman licked the established political machines, but today the big-business interests that he headed work in close co-operation with the Republican machine—they have a larger voice in the city's affairs than anywhere else in the state.

Tom Broderick, the Monroe County Republican chairman, is pretty openly the representative of big business. Decisions of the Rochester city administration are made, not in City Hall, but in the bank building a few hundred feet away, if important enough to be considered by the real powers. The University of Rochester is one of the most heavily endowed in the nation—third heaviest a few years ago. The leading morning and evening newspapers are both owned by Frank E. Gannett, about whose conservatism there can be no doubt. The Gannett newspapers print large quantities of national and world news in a much more objective fashion than most of the newspapers of the nation, but on local affairs they restrict themselves to a straight diet of sweetness and light. Eastman Kodak and Bausch & Lomb, the great optical-instrument makers, remained open-shop for years, and the only substantial organized labor force in the city was the Amalgamated Clothing Workers, employed in the city's renowned tailoring industry. The Democratic Party perks up in state and national campaign years, but plays dead the rest of the time.

The figures for Monroe County, including Rochester, are as follows:

ENROLLMENT

YEAR	DEMOCRATIC	REPUBLICAN	ALP
1944	51,162	154,678	3,844
1946	32,680	140,408	5,860

THE VOTE

YEAR	DEMOCRATIC	REPUBLICAN	ALP	LIBERAL
1944	108,973	111,725	9,584	1,116
1946	56,787	116,772	8,720	751

As can be seen, Roosevelt carried the county in 1944, with the help of the ALP and Liberal votes. His majority in the city of Rochester was approximately 20,000, but the enrollment figures, heavily weighted in favor of the Republicans, are a better guide to the vote on local candidates.

Buffalo, second largest city in the state, is a metropolis, or would be in any other state. It is nearly four hundred miles from New York City, and its politics are mysterious. It swings regularly from the Republican column into the Democratic and back again, without either party organization able to do much about it. Party factionalism and racial feelings run deep, and surface indications mean little. However, the Republican machine, headed by Edwin F. Jaeckle, former GOP state chairman, definitely runs Erie County, in which Buffalo is situated, and is thus in much better shape than the Democrats, who never can hope to win county control. The Democrats have been split by an intra-party fight that goes back to 1932 and has never healed. Buffalo has an extremely large Polish and German vote, particularly the former, and while the Buffalo Poles are normally Democratic, when they leave the ticket, as they did in 1946, the Democratic chances are nil.

Buffalo

Roosevelt carried the city for president by approximately 30,000 in 1944; Mead lost it for governor by 26,000 two years later. The figures for the county as a whole are:

ENROLLMENT

YEAR	DEMOCRATIC	REPUBLICAN	ALP
1944	153,132	207,205	5,606
1946	111,948	198,672	6,998

THE VOTE

YEAR	DEMOCRATIC	REPUBLICAN	ALP	LIBERAL
1944	176,554	185,975	17,735	1,616
1946	108,036	186,206	12,583	1,893

THE COUNTRY COUSINS

One of the favorite stories told about rural politics in New York—and it happens to be a true one—concerns a

Republican leader and legislator from central New York. One of his most faithful party workers was an Italian named Tony, who had come from Italy years before, spurned the city streets, and established himself up-state as a farmer and faithful GOP party worker. He farmed a good farm, raised many children; and every year he and his family cast and rounded up scores of votes for the good old GOP and for the leader, known to him as "Mr. Fred."

One day he went to Mr. Fred and asked for his first favor. Fred assured him anything he wanted would be granted. The farmer said: "Please, help me become a citizen."

The country vote is cast, in the main, by people who are citizens, whose grandfathers and great-grandfathers were citizens. It is the backbone of the Republican Party. The farm population dwindles with the years, and more and more of the up-state vote comes from the villages and the towns. But it remains Republican. A Democrat in many an up-state community is about as socially acceptable as a Republican in Mississippi.

There are good Republican organizations all over this section, and few in the Democratic ranks that count at all. In Binghamton, William H. Hill, an old-time leader, is the directing force of the party in the group of ten "southern tier" counties that lie along the Pennsylvania border. Hill's counties are good for a combined Republican majority of from 65,000 to 80,000 in any state-wide election.

And in the north country, the counties bordering on the St. Lawrence, whence comes much of the state's milk and dairy supplies, there is the Watertown organization that once ran the Republican Party in the state. It is to this day the most independent in its thinking of all the up-state organizations, principally on the issues of milk and water-power. Democratic candidates known to be on the side of the dairy farmer, as against the big milk companies, and for

146

the development of the St. Lawrence seaway and power project, run well ahead of their ticket in this area.

The Hudson River Valley counties seem to be above any such issues. They just vote Republican. Orange, Ulster, and Dutchess are places where the party's up-state majorities are nurtured. Franklin Roosevelt, born and bred in Dutchess, managed to carry the city of Poughkeepsie in one state landslide, but otherwise his neighbors voted against the man who was the county's chief claim to national fame. All gossip to the contrary, they would have voted just as solidly *for* him had he been a Republican.

One fact stands out in any study of the state, locality by locality. It is that the minority party's enrollment is always substantially smaller than its vote, while the majority-party enrollment is always larger than the vote it gets for its ticket. One obvious reason for this—but not the only reason —is that enrollment is a matter of public record, but the ballot is secret, and there are places all over the state where it pays to be known as a member of the majority party, whether one votes for its candidates or not.

No story about rural politics would be complete without the anecdote of the newspaperman, favorably remembered in his home county up-state, but carving out also a successful career in New York City. A friend of his who was caught in a Sunday "speed-trap" in the newspaperman's home town told him of the jam he was in, and the latter called the judge and asked for special consideration. The judge promised to take care of the case.

Some time later the newspaperman met the judge in New York City and asked him how his friend had made out. The judge smiled, and said:

"That was a funny one. You know, I forgot your friend's name, and I had to let all seventeen of them go free."

Chapter IX

COKE AND BLACKSTONE

Years ago Brooklyn had a traffic-court judge who cherished the vehicular code as if he had written it himself. His name was Fish. Magistrate Fish made no distinction between rich and poor or political friend and foe. He was feared and disliked for the fines and jail sentences he meted out to motorists. He never would consent to a "fix" or even to temper justice with mercy. Finally, the Democratic party organization nominated him for higher judicial office, merely to get him out of traffic court, where he was punishing too many good Democrats.

It is possible that if Fish had had to resign the first job to run for the second, the voters would have retired him from public life. But he didn't, and the public went determinedly into the polling places on election day and by a record majority elevated him out of the magistrate's court. It should be added that he made a very good civil-court judge; the traffic fines were lowered by his successor; an occasional favor was done for a friend; and everybody lived happily ever after.

It is moot whether this figures in political history as evidence for or against an elective judiciary as contrasted with the appointive system used in some states. Whatever the merits of that argument, up to the present nearly all judicial offices have been elective in New York State.

The public has shown a singularly constant apathy toward demands by reformers and legal highbrows that it give up its right to choose the men who sit in judgment on their legal problems, whether these problems be petty or great, simple or as involved as the law can be. The importance of the judiciary as the third arm of the government under the constitutional division of powers among the executive, legislative, and judicial branches reaches outside the state, for the decisions of the great judges who have sat in its high courts—Cardozo, Hiscock, and Pound, to name only three—have been copied by courts all over the Union, including the United States Supreme Court. The New York courts are important also for the vast volume of legal business they transact and for the money value of the issues decided.

The structure of the court system in New York is regarded throughout the nation as a model of simplicity and good governmental workmanship. As recently as 1947, neighboring New Jersey scrapped its hundred-year-old court structure and adopted New York's plan almost in its entirety, except for the election of judges.

While the New York courts dispense justice in a manner that is remarkably free from justifiable criticism, it is also true that the state judiciary is one of the most valuable assets of the two major political parties. The local party organizations in any county are more intimately concerned with the election of a state Supreme Court justice than they are with the Presidency of the United States, incredible as that may seem.

They make more noise campaigning for the latter, but there is more intra-organization rivalry over selecting the former. It is not that judges necessarily play politics in their judicial decisions—that is the exception rather than the rule—it is simply that the judiciary has immense favor and job patronage to dispense at all levels. A cabinet member can't take care of a traffic ticket the way a magistrate can. The job patronage that a president of the United States conceivably could allocate to any one county is negligible alongside of the list of receivers, referees, guardians, and administrators that a Supreme Court justice and a surrogate can appoint, from lists of lawyers supplied by the organization.

Tammany Hall, cut off from municipal patronage during La Guardia's twelve years in City Hall and also deprived of state and federal jobs by Lehman as Governor and Roosevelt as President, lived on the patronage given it by the judges it had nominated.

The top court in the state is the Court of Appeals, consisting of six associate judges and one chief judge, all elected in state-wide campaigns. It is the court of last resort in both civil and criminal cases unless a federal constitutional question happens to be involved, and then, of course, the United States Supreme Court has the final word.

All first-degree murder cases are automatically reviewed by the Court of Appeals, and it also possesses the unstated but unchallenged power to set aside acts of the state or local governments that infringe on the constitutional rights of the citizenry, the same way the United States Supreme Court does. In fact, it bears a remarkable resemblance to the Supreme Court in its deliberations. It is well removed from political control—despite the fact that its judges are elected—because the political leaders recognize that to tamper, or even appear to tamper, with the court would affront the public's conception of what is right and what is wrong.

Below the Court of Appeals, and not so far removed from politics, are the four Appellate Divisions of the Supreme Court, consisting of five or more justices from each of the four judicial departments of the state. Elected as Supreme Court justices, they are designated by the governor to hear appeals from the bench on which they were seated by the voters. There is a presiding justice of each Appellate Division, and he and his court share supervisory and administrative authority over the courts below.

Next in line is the Supreme Court, the basic civil court of the state system. Its members are elected from ten judicial districts—one, two, or three of which are included in each judicial department—into which the state is divided by the Constitution, the division having been fixed more or less on the volume of legal business. The Supreme Court is the highest court of original jurisdiction in the state, and while it has the right to handle criminal cases, it usually bothers only with civil actions involving reasonably large sums of money.

Still farther down on the lawsuit circuit are the city and municipal courts in New York City, equivalent lower courts in up-state cities, the justices of the peace in towns, and police justices in villages. They handle landlord and tenant litigation—the most tedious of all—squabbles over unpaid bills, damages to clothing sent to the cleaners and returned full of holes. Appeals from these lower civil courts go up the ladder through appellate terms of the Supreme Court— a subsidiary branch of the Appellate Division—in New York City and through the county courts elsewhere in the state.

Starting at the bottom on the criminal side, the lowest court in New York City is the magistrate's court, or police court, sometimes known up-state as recorder's court. The justices of the peace in towns and the police justices in villages are their rural equivalents, even though they handle civil cases too, as previously noted. They all take care of disorderly conduct, spitting in the subway, necking in parked cars, speeding, minor infractions of the peace. In New York City persons accused of slightly more serious offenses are remanded for trial to a special three-man court of super-magistrates, known as the Court of Special Sessions. And throughout the state, in cases of felonies, the low criminal courts hold the defendants for the grand jury. If the latter indicts, trial is by the county court.

In New York City the magistrates and special-sessions justices are appointed by the mayor; the justices of the peace and police justices up-state are elected. The people elect their county court judges too, one or more from each county. The county courts are the basic criminal courts in the same way that the Supreme Court is the basic civil court. In New York City the County Court judges get the same high pay that Supreme Court justices receive, while it varies elsewhere in the state. In the rural counties the salary is often small, and in a few places the judges are allowed to practice law on the side in their spare time. Starting with the surrogates and the county and supreme courts, the judges are elected for fourteen-year terms; judges of lower courts serve ten years as a rule.

On appeal, in criminal cases, the Appellate Divisions and the Court of Appeals are the final courts, just as they are in civil suits. There are other courts, too, like the Court of Claims, where the state may be sued and the judges are appointed by the governor, and the Family Courts, equivalent to specialized magistrates' courts. All told, there are more judges in New York State than one could shake a stick at if one dared. The total is well over 3,000, the size of a 1916 American infantry regiment. The last figures available break them up into details of 240 village police justices, 2,632 justices of the peace, 49 New York City magistrates, 34 surrogates, 125 Supreme Court and Appellate Division justices, 78 on the county courts, 7 on the Court of Appeals, and a few dozen more in assorted posts in the sixty-one other cities.

But from the point of view of the political organizations, there are only two courts of prime importance, the Supreme Court and the Surrogate's Court, the latter being the court which handles wills and administration of estates. One test of the importance of a political office is the number of men qualified for it who want it. A call for volunteers at a bar-association meeting to fill a vacancy on either of these courts would bring every man in the room to his feet, unless incumbents happened to be present. The man who made the offer of appointment would probably be trampled to death in the rush.

The salaries are comparatively high. The state gives a basic pay of $15,000 a year to its Supreme Court justices, with New York City putting up an additional $10,000 a year out of its own pocket to "insure" getting better men for the jobs inside the city limits. This was really good money up to a few years ago when the federal income tax was applied to judges. Now, even with a special cost-of-living increase, the judges' take-home pay is less than it formerly was. The surrogates in New York City receive the same pay as Supreme Court justices. Up-state it varies.

Despite the drop in income, however, the demand for places on the bench is just as great as it ever was, since it never really was the salary that attracted lawyers; most of those elected to the Supreme Court could or did earn more in private practice. But a high court nomination is still one of the supreme prizes a party organization can bestow.

It just seems that all lawyers, after a few years of looking up at judges while arguing the fine points of the law, acquire a secret ambition to exchange places with the men on the bench and make the rulings themselves. They crave the power and the glory of creating rules in connection with the ever changing law. They also like the security the bench affords. Any judge with a reasonably decent record of avoiding public scandal is fairly sure of renomination and re-election under existing practices.

The judges have to retire at the age of seventy under the provisions of the state Constitution that apply to all courts, but they get adequate pensions and are frequently appointed official referees, at two thirds their previous salary, to help out when court calendars are clogged.

The demand for judgeships by politically active lawyers being so great and the supply strictly limited, there is a black market in nominations. Men who have the political power to make a nomination have been known to sell it to the highest bidder from whom they deem it safe to take money. During the twenties the prospective judge simply paid the money into his party's campaign fund for party expenses, and those who excuse the appointment as an ambassador of a millionaire who has contributed liberally to the fund of the winning candidate for the Presidency, may justify such transactions in judgeships.

During the thirties, and notably in Manhattan, the cash was not paid into the coffers of the organization, but into the pockets of a few insiders, and the transactions came much closer to plain bribery. The price of a Supreme Court nomination at one time was as high as $100,000. When the federal tax on judicial salaries went into effect, the few political leaders who put judgeships on sale recognized the hard realities and shaved the price to approximately $70,-000.

Naturally, anyone putting up such a sum in advance of election does not do so merely for the privilege of running for office. Election must seem certain. But accidents happen, and in two cases in which the nominees suffered defeat through no fault of their own, they later got a second attempt at it without extra charge. The vast majority of judges mounted the bench by much more legitimate means, but the selling of judgeships does exist. When a complete unknown, without any record of party service and possessing no outstanding legal qualifications, appears as a party's nominee in an area where his election is a certainty, it is a fair deduction, based on known practices, that the bank

account of his family or a close friend has recently suffered
serious depletion.

There are political leaders all over the state who would
not sell a nomination, and there are countless lawyers who
would not buy one, no matter how much they wanted to sit
on the bench. Still, there are always a few with the ethics of
a certain lower-court judge who wanted to finish out his
career on the Supreme Court.

He was only six years away from the retirement age, however, so he offered his political leader six fourteenths of the
reputed market price, arguing that the job could be sold for
a full fourteen-year vacancy again in six years. The leader,
more practical than ethical, turned him down on the
ground that, with the uncertainty of politics, it was safer
to get the full price than it was to speculate on a resale six
years hence.

The fact that a place on the bench is bought now and
then is well known in political and legal circles. And while
lawyers are too polite to say so publicly, it is the real argument underlying drives by the bar associations and reform
groups to have the power of naming all high-court judges
placed in the hands of the governor. They feel that no
governor ever would be party to selling a job. They seem
to overlook the fact that a governor would be quite as likely
to accept the appointee offered by the dominant political
party in an area, providing it was also the governor's party,
as is the public, which now elects the judges. As to the
governor's responsibility for his appointments, he now has
the power to fill temporary vacancies, and as it has worked
out, he almost always accepts the recommendations of the
party leaders. The temporary appointment, in turn, pre-
sages the nomination of the appointee for a full-term election. Nothing in the procedure of over-all gubernatorial
appointment would prevent the sale of judicial office. It

might tend even to increase the number of very circumspect purchases.

It is interesting to note that in New York City the only scandals over deals in seats that have become public knowledge involved appointments of magistrates by Tammany mayors. Half a dozen federal judges have been convicted in different parts of the country for selling their courtroom judgments, and these were men holding lifetime appointments from the President of the United States. The greatest of these scandals involved Martin T. Manton, brilliant young jurist named years before to a high federal court by the upright and nonpolitical Woodrow Wilson. After twenty years on the bench he was convicted of selling his decisions on an over-the-counter basis. Ironically, in the same period not one of the state Supreme Court justices generally believed to have purchased his seat has ever been involved in a scandal related to his acts as a judge. This is not recorded in defense of the sellers of judgeships or of the ethics of lawyers who buy them. It may be only that few are more honest than reformed corruptionists.

The bar associations that want the governor to appoint all judges have another suggestion—that he pick the names from a panel presented by them rather than by the political leaders. The proposal is made by members of the legal profession who have a deep feeling about the sanctity of the bench and bar. But any move that took the nominating process away from the political parties and placed it in the hands of the leaders of the bar would have to be justified by the assumption that the bar associations did not play politics themselves, that they were free of political influence. That is not so.

In up-state New York the local political machines frequently control or influence the bar associations. In Brooklyn and the Bronx it is more than a coincidence that the candidates for judicial office of the Democratic Party are endorsed almost without exception by friendly bar groups, and that in Manhattan they are almost as uniformly opposed, or given a lukewarm reception, by a bar group dominated in its leadership by members of the opposite political party. In addition, the elements of logrolling and nepotism influence bar-association selections.

Another objection to the procedure suggested by the bar groups is that a community is entitled to a judiciary that is representative, just as it is entitled to a governor and a legislature that are representative, and the tendency of leaders of the legal profession to be conservative in their thinking would be reflected in the men they recommended for judicial appointment, regardless of the attitude of the voters. In the lower civil courts judges are notably responsive to public sentiment. For example, evictions became almost impossible to secure during the housing shortage. Even the Court of Appeals, like the United States Supreme Court, pays some attention to election returns—to public policy and welfare and not only to the purely legal aspects of a case. One recalls that when the constitutionality of a new charter for New York City was being argued before the Court of Appeals, a lawyer of great standing in the profession, who had been arguing against the charter, said to a friend: "I think I'm right on the law, but I know I'm going to lose the case. The court thinks the city needs a new charter, and that's all that counts." He lost the case.

Similarly, when the legality of the legislative reapportionment act of 1944 came before the court, it upheld the law, even though it had ruled out, on one technical ground or another, every previous reapportionment measure that had come before it over the years. The 1944 measure went farther in stretching the terms of the Constitution than any of the others, but by 1944 the state had not had a reapportion-

157

ment in twenty-seven years, and the Court of Appeals decided that the need was greater than the objections to the form of the bill.

Most of those on the bench in the state today are men who have worked their way up from the bottom, politically. They ran errands, they worked long and hard in connection with election matters, possibly as members and finally chairmen of the organization's law committee. They were aldermen, then Assemblymen, and then Congressmen. They did favors and made friends and finally were rewarded. They may have started in a lower court and have been promoted, rung by rung, all the way to the Appellate Division or the Court of Appeals. Such promotions are usually hailed by reformers and editorial writers as a welcome extension of the merit system. This may be, but to the organization such promotions are routine, obvious political mechanics. One vacancy on the Supreme Court can be made to furnish four political prizes. The first goes to the city court judge who moves up, the second to the municipal court justice who takes his place, the third to the assemblyman who gets the municipal court nomination, and the fourth to the man named to fill the Assembly vacancy thus created.

That sort of promotion is good for the morale of a political organization, and a good political boss will follow no other course. It keeps men on all levels of the political hierarchy hard at work in the hope of reward. The practice is common to up-state Republican political machines, to the O'Connell crowd in Albany, and to the Flynn machine in the Bronx and was the system of the successive McCooey, Kelly, and Cashmore leaderships in Brooklyn. A sure sign of decay in a machine is its stopping rewarding merit and starting selling preferment.

Since most judges get on the bench after years of training in practical politics, they retain their political awareness after election. It is true that there is a section of the state

Constitution forbidding high-court judges to run for other office, except other judicial office, without resigning. If this is supposed to keep the judges' minds off politics, it is remarkably ineffective. Even the judges who might have a tendency to immerse themselves purely in law don't get a chance. First of all, their secretaries and attendants are political appointees, suggested to them or named for them by the organization. The secretaryship to a Supreme Court justice or the chief clerkship of a court is commonly occupied by a district leader. Some of the latter regard the jobs as sinecures, and would resent being asked to work. Judges have been known to hire law secretaries out of their own pockets to do the work that must be done. On the other hand, many a judge of mediocre ability has been made to look good by the talent of the secretary foisted on him by the organization, and a really good secretary will be found writing opinions for several judges.

Some of the best secretaries have eventually landed on the bench themselves, put there through the influence of judges who desired to see faithful and competent workmen rewarded. One of the most brilliant of these, in addition to writing many a decision signed by another judge, also furnished the greatest mystery of the New York bench. His name was Joseph Force Crater, and his disappearance in the early thirties, soon after he reached the top of the heap politically with his election to the Supreme Court, has never been solved.

Apart from the actual court payrolls, the judges are kept in a constant state of awareness of the party organizations by the appointments they must make of referees, special masters, and so on. These appointments must go to lawyers, and a judge in making such an assignment usually can tell whether the duties involved or the importance of the case will justify a fat fee or a pittance. He appoints a lawyer from the list furnished him by the organization, though he retains, if he has any guts, the prerogative of demanding that the list contain the names of men capable of doing the job honestly and well.

In many counties and many courts the judges also have the power to designate the newspapers in which legal advertising appears. Many a public organ is kept friendly to a party organization through the legal advertising, it might be added. To a small paper that revenue has often represented the difference between black and red.

Sometimes judicial power can resolve an intra-party political fight. For example, in Tammany there was a bitter battle, starting in 1929, between John F. Curry, just put in as Tammany leader by Jimmy Walker, and the "Ahearn crowd," a group of old-line East Side leaders whom Walker did not like. Curry, acting for Walker, tried to drive them out of political life by starvation. Between 1929 and 1934 they got no jobs or favors from the organization, which controlled the entire county and city machinery. But the Ahearn crowd had one powerful friend, the Surrogate of New York County. He cut the Curry organization entirely off his patronage list, and gave its rival group enough sustenance to keep its ranks intact and in shape to take over the party—as it did when the Curry regime crumbled after the loss of the mayoralty to La Guardia. The Surrogate who thus used his power for strictly political purposes was not a political stumblebum, either. He was the late James A. Foley, probably the most effective, learned, and nationally respected jurist ever to spend his legal career on a purely local court. Foley, close associate of Al Smith and Bob Wagner, and son-in-law of Boss Murphy, could have been leader of Tammany Hall on Murphy's death; in fact, he was elected, but declined. He could have been mayor in place of Walker, and he still preferred the cloistered bench. But he never got politics out of his system.

It has been mentioned a number of times in this chapter

that the bosses pick the judges indirectly. Possibly a detailed explanation is in order. Magistrates and special-sessions justices are appointed by the mayor, but he accepts the recommendations of the county chairmen of his party, unless he happens to have other political fish to fry. Fiorello La Guardia, who accepted no dictation from any boss, kept half a dozen places empty on the magistrates' bench for almost a year before he left office. He used them for rewards to his friends just before he retired from the mayoralty.

Surrogates and County Court judges, as well as city and municipal court justices and their equivalents by slightly different names in up-state cities, are nominated directly in primary elections, and, as is noted elsewhere, the boss controls the primary or else he isn't boss. His candidates must be sure winners against any upstarts. Justices of the Supreme Court and judges of the Court of Appeals are named by judicial district and state conventions, the delegates to which are elected at the primary. But the slates of delegates filed by the machines are never contested, and rarely do the delegates to a judicial district convention even know whom they are going to vote for until "the word" is passed down the line by the boss's lieutenants. There have even been last-minute switches, when the party orator of the evening, while mounting the platform to make the nominating speech for one prospective judicial light has been handed a slip of paper giving him instructions to sing the praises of another.

There was the seriocomic case of a politician from Little Italy who had an appointment at City Hall to be sworn in as a city magistrate at two p.m. On the dot he arrived at City Hall, accompanied by two brass bands and several hundred of his countrymen who had paraded with him all the way. On time as he was, he was too late to witness the swearing in, by the Mayor, of a rival for the post.

In one judicial district there are politicians who still

chuckle over a political unknown who was very nearly handed to the electorate under the wrong name. His name was something like Russell George and only an accidental reminder kept the convention from nominating George Russell. But with all the demerits of the present system of naming judges, the public at least usually has had the choice between nominees of the two major parties and it has been known to exercise that choice with intelligence. It is not able to defeat a hack candidate in a year when the tide is running completely with the party of that nominee, but it has turned up its nose at machine candidates often enough to keep the judiciary in reasonably good shape.

The party leaderships, however, in recent years have worked out a new wrinkle that looks all right on the surface, but is inherently bad. This is the system of bipartisan endorsements. It started out modestly enough, and on a sound basis, applied to judges completing a full term on the bench. Any judge who did that without discredit became entitled by custom to re-election without a contest, through endorsement of all parties. The public repeatedly showed its approval of this and disapproval of anything to the contrary. It amounts to a guarantee of tenure up to the mandatory retirement age of seventy.

But both parties in recent years have shown a desire to expand the bipartisan-endorsement theory for their own purposes, to capitalize on public approval of the original idea and also to take advantage of the failure to understand the harm in extending it. Suppose there are three vacancies on the Supreme Court in the First Judicial District, which includes Manhattan and the Bronx, to be filled because of deaths or retirements. Suppose also that the Republicans have a candidate they are extremely anxious to see on the bench, but know they can't elect him, regardless of his qualifications, in that predominantly Democratic area. The Democrats have some candidates, of only fair legal repute, whom they could elect in a straight Democratic-Republican fight. The minor parties, however, might combine with the Republicans if the Democrats made no concessions to them. So the Democratic and Republican leaders get together and, without even mentioning the names of the men they will select to fill their respective quotas, divide the places on a two-for-one basis. The public is then confronted with a two-party ticket, which the leaders try to sell as "non-partisan," consisting of two Democrats and one Republican running as the three Democratic nominees and the same trio running also as the Republican nominees. The votes cast on both party lines are lumped in computing the result; the combination is unbeatable and the election unnecessary for practical purposes.

That is exactly what happened in the much publicized Aurelio case in 1943. Thomas A. Aurelio, a city magistrate, was one of two Democratic nominees accepted blindfold by the Republicans in return for the Democratic nomination of David W. Peck, Governor Dewey's choice. Peck, a brilliant lawyer, was later made presiding justice of the Appellate Division by Dewey. Aurelio, with nothing on his prior record as a city magistrate that could be held against him, has since held his place on the Supreme Court without criticism.

But right after the nominations were made, Aurelio had the questionable judgment to call up the *padrone* who had helped him get the nomination, one Frank Costello, a figure of considerable importance in the underworld. No one ever suggested that Aurelio paid for his nomination—the indications were all to the contrary—but Costello's wire was tapped, for other reasons, by the police, and Aurelio's profuse thanks to the underworld character did not make pretty reading when a transcript of the conversation was made public by the District Attorney. And the Governor and the bar associations seized on the incident as a conspicuous example of the evil inherent in electing, rather than appointing, judges. What they overlooked was that the procedure in the Aurelio case, to which the Governor was a party, was not an election; it was a conspiracy to prevent an election.

The Democrats and the Republicans "disowned" Aurelio after the tapped-wire conversation was made public, and the Democrats theoretically threw their weight behind the American Labor Party nominee, while the Republicans sponsored still another independent candidate. But Aurelio wore both official labels on the election ballot, and the disunited opposition could not defeat him, though he did not receive a majority of the votes cast. The leader of Tammany Hall who nominated Aurelio and then tried to disown him was booted out shortly afterward, not because he was responsible for the nomination, but because he backed water when it hit stormy seas.

Probably the principal weakness in the state's judicial system was cleared up by constitutional amendment in 1947. Up to then lower-court judges were removable by the appellate division of the department in which they served, but County or Supreme Court justices could be kicked off the bench only by the Legislature under a complicated impeachment procedure. The Legislature, full of lawyers, showed consistent reluctance over the years to exercise its impeachment powers. The 1947 change provided an alternate method, permitting the setting up of a special court composed of high-ranking members of the judiciary itself to act on complaints.

In appraising the New York judiciary, one can always keep one's perspective by remembering the two Judges Cardozo. Benjamin Nathan Cardozo was a great jurist, possibly one of the greatest. His record on the Court of Appeals and later on the United States Supreme Court was outstanding, his knowledge of the law was infinite, and his character irreproachable. The other Judge Cardozo was his father, Albert, removed from office because he was a leading member of the Tweed Ring, the most corrupt crew ever exposed in the state's history.

Chapter X

THE LAWMAKERS

The Democratic Party won every biennial election in New York State from 1930 through 1940; and in the decade preceding, the party elected a Governor four times out of five. Yet in only one year in those twenty were the Democrats able to carry both houses of the state Legislature, the members of which were chosen at that same series of elections.

This was not accidental, nor is it unique to New York State. In nearly every state where there is a political division existing between the cities and the rural areas, there is some sort of "rotten borough" system that stacks the cards of representation against the city populations in favor of the country areas. In some states we find the principal city with only one representative in one of the houses of the Legislature, since the members of that house are apportioned to a county, regardless of population. In New York the situation is not that bad, but neither is there equal representation.

New York operates under a system of legislative apportionment written into the state Constitution in 1894 by a group of smart up-state Republicans who saw that some day New York City would have a majority of the population of the state and were determined it should never have a majority of the Legislature.

So each of New York's 62 counties was forever guaranteed representation by at least one member of the Assembly, no matter how small the population of the county, and the membership of that lower and supposedly popular house was fixed forever at 150. An exception was made for two counties in the wilds of the Adirondacks, Fulton and Hamilton, which for legislative representation may be regarded as one. In the case of the state Senate, upper branch of the Legislature, it was simply provided that no two counties divided by a river—New York and Kings (Brooklyn) were in mind—could ever have half the Senate seats. There are other clauses, too, aimed at preserving up-state control if not completely rural domination. One of these makes the basis of apportionment "citizen population" as contrasted with congressional apportionments based on the entire population.

Operating under the 1894 constitutional mandate, the Legislature itself draws the actual apportionment measures. One adopted in 1917 appeared to ensure rural control, but the character of the population changed in several areas, and by 1944, when a new bill was passed, the Democrats had proved that they sometimes could win control of the Senate, if they were carrying the state by landslide or near-landslide proportions for other offices.

In 1944 the Legislature passed, and the courts upheld, an apportionment bill that added five seats to the state Senate, mostly for the benefit of the suburban counties adjacent to New York City.

It left New York City, possessed of a clean majority of the state's population, with 25 of the 56 seats in the Senate, and 67 of the 150 seats in the Assembly. In addition, the individual district lines were drawn in or around the counties to favor the Republicans.

In 1944, at the first legislative election held under the new and supposedly equalized division of legislative seats, the Democrats elected 21 members of the Senate against 35 for the Republicans, and 55 members of the Assembly against 94 Republicans and one American Labor Party member. In the presidential choice that same day the Democrats carried the state by a majority of 315,000.

So it appears that now and for many years to come the Senate and the Assembly will be safely tucked away in the Republican election basket no matter how the vote goes for other offices. This will be true until acquisition of half-acre estates ceases to make suburbanites conservative and until the farmers and the villagers forsake the Republican Party they have supported since the Civil War.

This happened once in modern political history. The candidacy of Robert Moses for governor on the Republican ticket in 1934, coming in a year when the party's fortunes nationally were at a low ebb, kept the GOP up-state voters away from the polls in droves. Others voted Democratic to register further resentment toward their party. The Democrats carried the Governorship by a majority of 808,000 and won the Assembly by a margin of one vote, 76 to 74. They already had the Senate from the Hoover debacle of 1932.

But barring a freakish upset like the 1934 election, the system of legislative apportionment in the state means that the state can have a governor and a legislature controlled by the same party only if the state happens to elect a Republican governor, as it did in the Harding landslide of 1920 and again in 1942 and 1946. In the nation, when the President and Congress are of different parties or if one controls the House and the other the Senate, there is much talk of governmental stalemate and even demands for constitutional revision. In the state it is taken as a matter of course, and it is probably more than a coincidence that the periods of divided control have produced some of the best governing and the best legislating the state has ever known.

Al Smith never had a legislature of his own party during his four terms as Governor, and while Al campaigned for his supporters at every election, he never really wanted

168

them in the legislative majority, no matter what he said for the record. Roosevelt as Governor held similar views, and Herbert H. Lehman, who had a Legislature of his own party for the session of 1935, wiped his brow when the boys went home, and uttered a silent wish for the GOP to take back the lawmaking machinery. The Republicans obliged at the fall elections, and for the next seven years the Governor was able to damn the Legislature for its shortcomings with a clear conscience and no party qualms.

It is axiomatic in politics that it is much easier to damn the opposition villains than those of one's own party, the latter being a handicap to tactics and a gag on the vocal organs. Thus Smith, Roosevelt, and Lehman, blessed with opposition Legislatures, were able to hammer away in support of state-wide policies they knew were popular with the people, or could be made popular. For a time—in fact, for the whole period required to build up Smith and Roosevelt into presidential contenders—the Republican leaders in the Legislature and the state were not quite bright about this. They would start out in opposition. Then Smith or his successors would take the case to the people over the radio or in stump speeches, and the GOP legislative leaders would give in, not because the Governor could bring about their defeat at the polls as individuals, but because of the effect further obstructionism would have on their party's chances of carrying the state for governor or president in the next election.

More and more during the Lehman administrations the Republican leadership withheld taking a stand on proposals by the Democratic Governor until it had had a chance to weigh the state-wide political consequences. But whether it was early or late, the Legislature usually went along with the Governor on measures for the good of the people, or at least those capable of political dramatization. So the Legislature, elected on a basis of representation designed to circumvent the mass of the people, has in practice listened to them. Its record, over a period of years, seems more consistently representative of the wishes of the majority of the people than does that of Congress.

The Legislature consists of 150 members of the Assembly and 56 members of the Senate at the present writing. Both houses are elected now for two-year terms. The Assembly had its tenure increased from one year to two by constitutional amendment in 1938, the same time the term of the Governor was increased from two years to four. The Senators have sought longer tenure, too, but up to now their efforts to get it increased to four years have been blocked by the quiet opposition of the local leadership of both major parties.

District and county leaders who pick state Senators are themselves elected for only two-year terms by their party followers. Their feeling is that neither they nor the leadership of their party in the state or in the Legislature would be able to control the Senators if the latter had to run for renomination and re-election only once in four years.

That control, by the legislative leadership in particular— a tight control of the kind that has not been seen in Congress since the days of Uncle Joe Cannon—has been an important key to the relative success of the state Legislature. The legislators are not robots, but the rule of the leadership, overriding the whims or personal desires of members, has meant that on *important* issues, involving the passage of good bills or the killing of bad ones, members can be coerced, if necessary, into voting the way the welfare of the party or the state as a whole dictates.

There is no drama in routine legislating, and most of the legislative stories worth repeating therefore concern the extreme, the unusual situation. For example, in 1938 Governor Lehman sent to the Legislature a recommendation that the insurance law be changed to permit savings banks to issue up to $3,000 of life insurance to their depositors, with the premiums deducted automatically from their pass-book balances. It was a cheap form of insurance and the regular insurance companies, which could not compete, were against the bill. The banks were lukewarm about it. The Assembly at the time was under Republican control and the Senate under Democratic. The Assembly leadership, knowing that the measure was one that the Governor could make popular with the people if it were the GOP that refused to enact it, sent word that if the Democratic Senate passed the bill, the Republican Assembly would drum into line the votes needed to make it a law.

The insurance lobby had the measure bottled up in committee in the Senate. A group of Democratic Senators, for reasons of their own, were listening to the insurance-company arguments rather than to those of their own Governor. By a vote in committee, the bill was killed. It was dead for the session, so far as legislative precedent and procedure were concerned. But John Dunnigan, the Democratic majority leader, proceeded to override that committee with a complete and impertinent disregard for that precedent and procedure. Armed with just another printed copy of the bill —not the original copy—plus a blank committee roll-call, Dunnigan cornered every Democrat on the committee separately and ordered him to sign as approving the measure.

Each protested. They had just voted the other way. The committee couldn't reverse itself, especially without even having a meeting, each one said in turn.

"Who's leader around here, you or me?" Dunnigan stormed. "Sign, I said, sign." They signed. Dunnigan ignored the committee chairman and personally reported the bill out on the floor. The Senate passed it and so did the Assembly. Of course, if the Republican Assembly had been willing to throttle the bill, Dunnigan would never have had to bully his Senators into voting for it. They would have done so gladly, fortified by the knowledge that it would not become law and that both their civic obligations to their constituents and whatever obligations they had to the insurance lobby would have been fulfilled.

Many newspaper readers form their impression of the Legislature from feature stories on the introduction of bills of the screwball variety and outrageously radical or reactionary measures. Few of these are introduced with serious intent; for the most part they are offered to please a constituent here, a pressure group there, and the Legislature usually kills them in committee. Those that do emerge from committee are taken care of by the more complicated procedure of buck-passing.

That popular Assemblyman, Joe Zilch, of Ossawattomie County, whose baritone would be missed at late Monday night parties if he ever were turned down for renomination, has a bill some important folk back home want enacted. Joe knows it won't work, but he can't tell that to the people who contribute cash or doorbell-ringing to his campaign every election year.

Nor would it do for Joe to confess he hadn't enough influence in the Assembly to put the bill through. He explains his problem to the legislative leadership and receives sympathetic understanding; his bill passes the Assembly unanimously in the closing hours of a three-month session. The minority does not even ask for a roll-call. But somehow the measure gets lost in the rush in the Senate. It never comes out of committee. Joe returns happily to Ossawattomie and tells the boys how he passed the bill, but "that damn Senate . . ."

The Assembly acts with similar courtesy in disposing of some of the legislative turkeys for Senators who have constituency trouble. Usually, that is. One year when the Senate was passing everything in the sublime assurance that the Assembly would bury the smelliest measures, Speaker Oswald D. Heck picked up the telephone and called Joe R. Hanley, then the Senate majority leader. He told Hanley that if the Senate passed and continued to send over that kind of legislation—he used a shorter and more descriptive word—the Assembly would pass it too, and how would the Senate like that? The flood slowed down.

While the tendency of one house of the Legislature to pass the buck to the other may be condemned in theory, it works well in practice and is, at least to me, a valid argument against a unicameral legislature of the type in existence in Nebraska. Under the bicameral system, one house may pass a bad bill, and if there is public outcry, the other house can kill the measure without anyone's losing caste.

It is true that the Legislature functions at its worst on items involving no gubernatorial signature or veto. One of these is the passing of resolutions, of no binding legal effect, and usually petitioning Congress to do something that the Legislature itself would never consider doing. Many of the resolutions are silly, and none represents mature consideration.

Some day a legislative leadership with a sense of humor will push through both houses resolutions calling for the abolition of their own legislative bodies and the speedy execution of the members. If read in the usual mumbling tone by the clerk and voted on in the usual uninquiring manner, the resolution will be adopted unanimously.

The legislators also give only superficial consideration to proposed constitutional amendments, though under the Constitution the procedure was designed to call for real study. After the first adoption of a constitutional change a legislative election must intervene, so that the people can turn thumbs down on the men who voted for it if they care to, and then the amendment must go before the Legislature again. If it is approved a second time, the people vote on it at the following general election. Instead of taking their role in the Constitution-making process seriously, the legislators take the attitude that since the people will pass on the measure in the end and therefore are the final authority, the legislators are merely passing on whether to permit a referendum and not on the substance of the amendment.

There is one major difference between the New York Legislature and Congress in the procedure of passing a bill. In Congress the House can pass one bill and the Senate another; then a compromise measure is worked out by a a conference committee for approval by both houses. In the state the identical bill must be voted by both houses; all steps to make conflicting measures identical are taken unofficially, and when the Senate, for example, considers an Assembly bill, it does so by courtesy of the Senate sponsor of the companion measure, who formally moves on the floor to substitute the Assembly measure for his own bill.

The Assemblyman exercises similar courtesy toward the Senator on another bill, and if they get into a jam, it is the job of the party leadership to straighten it out. In order to understand the relationship between legislator and legislative leaders, between the legislator and party policy, one simply has to remember that the Assemblyman is elected from a district, usually small in area and never larger than one county, that he must run for nomination as well as election, and that therefore he must be on good terms with his county chairman and his district boss. That is true also of the State Senator, except that the area he runs in is larger.

Fred Young, of Lewis County, was one state Senator who was frequently independent of his legislative leadership and of the leadership of the party in the state, but he never disagreed with his county chairman. After he received orders from the majority leader to vote for a measure he did not like, he would go through the motions of calling his home town and would emerge from the telephone booth saying he had been in conference with his county chairman, and his chairman had told him to vote against the leadership on the bill. Young, of course, was county chairman of Lewis County.

There were and are a few others in an equally fortunate political position, but in normal cases, on issues of importance, the county chairman can influence a legislator to vote for or against a measure, applying the pressure either by himself or at the request of the party leadership. In the Assembly the speaker appoints the members and the chairman of all the committees. He runs the Rules Committee, and the Rules Committee runs the Assembly in the all-important closing weeks of a session. The same is true in the Senate, with the power resting in the hands of the majority leader. During a session they see a lot of the county chairmen, who drop in at Albany to secure the passage of legislation important back home. Maybe an important local industry, good for a substantial campaign contribution, has a problem that a little bill can solve. The speaker or the majority leader acts as a clearing house on such requests. He steers through to passage all that he reasonably can.

A successful legislative leader knows that in a pinch these same county chairmen will reciprocate and use hometown pressure to keep wandering legislators in line and on hand to vote the way the speaker desires. In addition, the speaker wins the personal loyalty of the individual members by the tact and care with which he handles their individual problems. The threads of responsibility, running from the localities and the state leadership of the party, all pass through the hands of the legislative leadership.

In each house in Albany there is a center aisle sharply dividing the legislative chamber. Looking down from the rostrum, the Republicans are seated to the left of the line and the Democrats to the right. The line is more than physically present. It is the line of party regularity, too. The leader of each house knows that at any time, by calling for a "party vote," his floor whip can furnish him enough support from his side of the aisle to pass any bill. If there are any bolters from the majority on a party-vote roll-call, their total, registered by a scattered show of hands, is merely deducted from the official number of the majority party elected to that house and the bill is declared passed, providing that the majority has been big enough in the first place. Most bills are passed by "short" roll-calls, with only the names of the first and last members, alphabetically, called along with those of the majority and minority leaders. No attempt is made to get a detailed vote. On this type, the dissenters are deducted from the entire membership of the house, and a vote of 135 to 15 is possible with only 90 members present in the Assembly. A report on legislative practices in 1945 showed the Senate passed 1,482 out of 1,660 bills that way, while the score in the Assembly was 1,403 out of 1,603.

In Congress a bill is passed by a mere majority of those present as long as there is a quorum. In the state the Constitution says flatly that no bill can become a law unless it receives a majority of the votes of the members elected to each house, present or not. So 76 affirmative votes are needed in the Assembly and 29 in the Senate. Usually the votes are either there or so close at hand that the clerks are not too fussy about an exact count.

At least once that system of the counting by the clerk has backfired. A bill had slipped out of the Rules Committee, escaping the watchful eye of the speaker, who was against it. The clerk, operating on the normally sound theory that a bill that emerges from the Rules Committee is favored by the majority, called the roll and announced the result as ayes 76, nays 49. There were not that many votes in the chamber at the time, but the Democrats did not challenge him. The speaker, however, gave the sign to a majority member, and the legislator duly rose to announce he was changing his vote from aye to nay. Not even that bothered the clerk. Ayes 76, nays 50, he announced as the corrected result. The speaker gave up.

On another occasion when the roll-call did not reflect accurately the sentiments of those present, the measure was a really important one involving Dewey's prestige. He had told the leaders it must be passed. The powerful teachers' lobby was opposing the bill and had mustered solid Democratic and scattering Republican support. The bill came up at two a.m. the morning the Legislature was adjourning, and the GOP did not have on hand the 76 votes to pass it. It had, to be exact, 74, excluding the speaker, who votes only when his vote is needed. But the clerk announced the result as ayes 77, nays 63. The Democrats stormed the rostrum, demanding a detailed recount. The speaker announced he was voting for the bill, making the real total 75. Then there was some hasty whispering across the center aisle between the Democratic floor leader and the Republican floor leader, and the former withdrew his protest. The bill was declared passed.

What Irving Ives, the majority leader, had whispered to Irwin Steingut, the minority leader, was that one Republican had sneaked away in advance of adjournment to his home in Westchester County, and if the Democrats insisted on the recount, the Republican leadership would keep the house in session for the eight to ten hours it would take to send a sergeant at arms down to Ossining, where the member lived, and bring him back, under arrest if necessary, to cast his vote. Party discipline, exercised in this case by the speaker and aided by the pressure from the Governor, was going to pass the bill somehow, and Steingut, an experienced legislator, saw no reason why everybody should be kept up the rest of the night merely for the postponing of the inevitable.

During the Dewey administrations, with the Governor

and the Legislature of the same party, much of the disciplining of members for party purposes passed into the hands of the Governor. He issued his orders on legislation and the majority members accepted them, though often grumblingly.

A governor, whether the Legislature is run by his own party or not, has a check on it that should be the envy of the President of the United States. No legislature within the memory of anyone now around Albany has ever passed a bill over a governor's veto, even though the Legislature enjoys the same right as Congress to override a veto by a two-thirds vote. In the first place, no party ever attains a two-thirds majority in both houses without getting the Governorship as well, and on the issue of overriding a governor party lines would hold tighter than on any other. This is so thoroughly accepted that there have been no attempts one can remember even to bring a vetoed bill to a second vote.

Many bills passed in Albany every session are of importance only to small groups or to small localities. The general welfare of the state is not involved, neither is the political prestige of the two major parties. Sometimes the content of bills is so technical or the interest so limited that they are not mentioned in the newspapers when introduced or adopted. Yet the bills mean something to their legislative sponsors. If they come from legislators who have been helpful, the Governor may sign the bills. With an equally clear conscience he may veto them. In either case the action usually comes after the Legislature has gone home—the Governor has thirty days in which to act on measures passed during the last ten days of a session—and his action, either way, provides a powerful incentive for co-operation with the Governor, even for members of the opposite political faith.

Within his own party the Governor has the power to

make affirmative awards to ambitious members looking for prestige in their legislative careers. He usually has a legislative program that is fairly certain of enactment into law or that at least will attract newspaper comment and attention. It goes into the legislative hoppers, not in the name of the Governor, but in the names of individual legislators. They vie for the honor of introducing such legislation, and the honor does not go to party rebels.

It should be obvious that there would not be the need for the Governor to exercise constant control, or to have it done for him by the legislative leaders and county chairmen, if the legislators themselves were simply a flock of sheep. They aren't. There are a few sheep and just as many rugged individualists. In between is the largest group, which sometimes follows and sometimes breaks away. There are legislators of brilliance and of mediocrity; there are serious workers and blatherskites, honest men and dishonest men, in just about the same percentages as men of these characteristics in the population as a whole. Any small difference in percentage probably favors the Legislature.

There are also playboys, who nightly take in all of Albany's limited entertainment features. And there are members who go to a movie and then go to bed. A few read all legislation and know exactly what they are voting on every time. The vast majority realizes that it is just as easy to follow the lead of the few "specialists" on each major state problem, and they vote aye or nay on the basis of how the measure is presented to the membership on the floor, unless party considerations dictate otherwise.

Up to 1947, when a constitutional amendment permitted the Legislature to fix its own future pay—and it set it at $5,000—the legislators were paid $2,500 a year by the state, a figure that was high compared with that of other states. They also received travel expenses. To the retired farmer or grain and seed merchant from an up-state hamlet this salary was enough to pay him for his time. To the urban lawyer or insurance agent it was chicken-feed—about enough to pay his entertainment expenses during a dull session.

Despite the low pay, the latter always have figured that membership in the Legislature gave them business contacts. For lawyers, apart from immediate legal fees or patronage, there is always the hope that faithful service will bring a nomination to the bench, the ambition of most men in the legal fraternity. Some members, who went originally to Albany for no reason in particular, stay on and on just for the friendships they have made. The Albany scene is a warm one; a spirit of live and let live, of genuine tolerance, pervades the membership—all members of a club and all living away from home—and many simply hate to leave a place of such spirit. Even those who do leave come back yearly for the annual dinner of the legislative correspondents, just to renew old friendships and rehash old stories.

It is only at the tail end of a session that being a legislator becomes a full-time job for the average member. The Legislature convenes regularly on a Monday night—the lawyers can even answer court calendars Monday morning and catch midafternoon trains for the Capitol—and there are sessions on Tuesday and possibly Wednesday during the early weeks. Only noncontroversial bills are enacted after Tuesday for many weeks during the session, and a full five-day working week is not the rule until the last two weeks before the tentative adjournment date.

For the legislative leaders the situation is different. Their jobs, if they really do justice to them, are full-time, all-year occupations. In the Assembly these leaders are the speaker, the majority and minority leaders, and the chairman of the Ways and Means Committee. In the Senate they are the majority and minority leaders, and the chairman of the Finance Committee. They have research staffs and function informally the way formal legislative councils operate in some other states. They have to worry about the upkeep of state institutions, about plans for the future, as much as the Governor and his state department heads. Acting in concert with the Governor, they have authority to appropriate money when the Legislature is not in session, giving their pledge, on a note, that the two houses will pick up the I O U by a regular appropriation bill when they reconvene. The lobbies and pressure groups are on their necks whether the Legislature is in session or not.

In return for this, prior to the 1947 constitutional amendment, they received "lulus." This was Al Smith's way of describing money paid out "in lieu of" expenses. The legislative leaders received "lulus" ranging from $7,500 to $9,000 a year over their basic salaries so that they could live comfortably and not begrudge the time their jobs require. While the money was given in the form of expenses, as a subterfuge, they paid taxes on it as income. The 1947 amendment legalized additional payments to the leaders.

The question of corruption, of the "little black bag," has plagued the Legislature but little in modern times. In the first decade of the century there was a bipartisan troop of legislative bandits who would gang up on some industry and charge it a good round sum in unmarked bills either for passing some needed legislation or for not passing a proposed measure that might put it out of business. Eventually publicity and the attitude of Charles Evans Hughes as Governor dispersed the crew, and it is probable that cash on the line as a *quid pro quo* for the passing or killing of a bill has not been paid out in years. There may be long-range payoffs of another variety, but crude bribery is obsolete.

The Legislature has had unnecessary employees, who came to Albany just once a month to draw their pay. This was particularly true when the Republicans were out of power in the state and nation and needed a little legislative payroll padding to eke out their county patronage require-ments. The Democrats winked and took a minority share.

When Dewey was elected Governor, he began a drive against the O'Connell organization in Albany, to weaken it, to break it up if possible. The machine threatened to re-taliate with an investigation of legislative funds and pay-roll padding, carried out by the Democratic District At-torney of Albany County, home site of whatever crimes had been committed.

The Governor balked this by superseding the District Attorney, naming his own prosecutor to carry on the probe, and turning a proposed Democratic investigation of Repub-licans into a Republican investigation of the Democrats. The probe failed to convict any major scapegoats, but it did result in eliminating a few drones, at least temporarily.

For good or for bad, Dewey exercised his actual and tit-ular party leadership with a vengeance. First he established a system of "pre-veto." This meant simply that the Gover-nor never had to act at all, officially, on any bill that might be embarrassing if it reached him for signature or veto. The bills were sized up and discussed in conference with the legislative leadership before they were acted upon in the legislative committees. If the Governor did not want to act on a bill, it was ordered killed in legislative committee, and it was. In the first two years of the Dewey regime only one measure ordered slaughtered under the pre-veto system was sent to the Governor, and that went with the connivance of legislative leaders, who were momentarily irked by too rigid a supervision. There have been no recorded uprisings of a similar nature since. A member of the Rules Committee who publicly and literally held his nose as he voted for a Dewey measure was quietly denied renomination by his county chairman the following fall. A little investigation into the personal past of another member, and he stopped being obstreperous. Despite the single revolt, the system worked so well in the first two years that the Governor's power has not been challenged since.

While the majority is thus held in check, what about the minority? What can they do about anything? The answer is: little. Theoretically they always can move to have a committee discharged from further consideration of a measure and to bring it out on the floor for debate. But no such move ever succeeds, since even a sympathetic majority member will not vote to override the committee. The minority knows this and is simply trying for a record vote, to be used as campaign material in the next election. But even that is sometimes futile, since the majority members can always claim they were not opposed to the bill but merely to the parliamentary device being employed. The bill is debated, on a motion to discharge, but legislative debate gets short shrift in the newspapers against the competition of world affairs.

Sometimes measures come up in the Legislature on which the party in control takes a definite stand that would seriously embarrass a few of the members in their home districts if they went along with their party. This is particularly true of measures affecting New York City which city Republicans may feel they have to favor, but which their party opposes. If the majority happens to have the votes to spare to pass the bill anyhow, these members are quietly "excused" from voting with their party and allowed to join the opposition ranks. Everyone understands this is no major revolt, that the members in question have not suddenly become renegades.

In return for all the loyalty and votes the members give the leadership during the course of a session, they expect one main thing: that promises to them will be kept. One speaker of the Republican majority failed to do that, a number of years ago, in the opinion of about eight of his followers. When the next session opened, they voted as a bloc for another candidate for speaker, deadlocking the election, since their defection reduced the Republicans below the majority level. The deadlock continued for weeks until another speaker acceptable to all factions was decided on.

In general, the Legislature moves slowly. Practically all its work involves changing something already on the statute books rather than the enactment of something new. It is constantly amending the rules of the game as these apply to some particular group or industrial and economic force. Good bills may be passed for poor motives and bad ones from good intentions. And bills are even passed by accident.

One year a Republican legislator, well-intentioned but habitually ineffective, sponsored a pretty fair piece of legislation that the Democrats, in control of the Senate, had no intention of enacting. After all, there was no hurry about it, and they could introduce it themselves next year and get the credit, if they decided that was the politic thing to do. But three days before adjournment the Republican Senator was taken to the hospital for an emergency operation. While he was flat on his back, the Senate passed his bill. "I thought it might help him get well," Dunnigan explained with a grin.

Aside from such incidents, one cannot examine the work of the Legislature over a period of years without concluding that it has been more responsive to public needs and public opinion than most legislative bodies, including Congress. It is still too early to tell what will be the effect of the recently renewed guarantee written by the 1944 apportionment bill that neither house of the Legislature can ever go Democratic—can ever be lost by the Republicans. The leadership, possessed on one side of the certainty of continued control, and on the other of a permanent place in the doghouse, may get sloppy and careless. The individual members are likely to continue to vote as they have in the past. This involves keeping one eye on their party leadership, the other on their personal inclinations, and both ears to the ground.

Chapter XI

THE MAN IN THE MANSION

Men have been known to rule themselves out of consideration for the Presidency of the United States, or to have been eliminated by their party, because they were not able physically to handle the task. They were too old or too ill to stand the grind of the biggest administrative and policy-making job on earth. Other men, of equal or lesser attainments, have declined to consider being mayor of New York City because of the headaches involved.

There is no known case of anyone refusing to become Governor of New York, or refusing to seek the post, for those reasons. Compared with the Presidency or the mayoralty—and the statement must be considered in the purely relative sense in which it is offered—the Governorship is a soft snap. Save in rare emergencies, the press of work is not much greater than that on any big-business executive. The physical strain is light enough so that any man of sound mind and sound politics, with the ability to pick trustworthy subordinates, can function adequately as governor.

The reason for this is simply that the important part of the job of governor lies in the field of policy-making rather than in the handling of administrative detail. The Governor is not wakened late at night or early in the morning by recurrent crises in international affairs, nor is his executive domain so vast that the number of minutes in the calendar week is insufficient to permit even abbreviated conversations with each of his lieutenants, a difficulty which plagues a modern President.

The Governor does not have to work overtime every time a snowstorm blocks streets and delays garbage collection, as does a mayor of New York City; nor does every strike called or threatened land in his lap for settlement. He has his office in the State Capitol and half a dozen blocks away his mansion on Eagle Street, where he can relax or work as he sees fit, without a constant stream of visitors. In addition to this immediate privacy, he has one other priceless advantage over the Mayor of New York City. His own relative isolation in Albany means that the strain of attending four or five public dinners a night can be avoided.

The fact that the major requirement of a governor is skill in policy-making makes the post attractive from two viewpoints. First, it is not as boresome with its details as the mayoralty would be if a mayor ever had time to get bored. Secondly, it is policies rather than details that get newspaper headlines and have made the Governorship of New York State, rather than the bigger administrative job of Mayor of New York City, the natural stepping-stone to the Presidency.

The only Mayor of Greater New York who was ever a possibility for high national office was La Guardia, who might have gone far if he had been a political regular and thus had a party to support him. Al Smith, who could have been elected Mayor of New York at any time without substantial opposition, refused that job when a citizens committee, in 1933, asked him to run. Al was not looking for further political troubles. Tom Dewey, asked one evening whether he intended to take any action in a complicated New York City situation, looked at the reporter and smilingly replied:

"I was elected Governor last fall [1946], not Mayor."

The Governor's job in general is a comfortable one and

it has its emoluments. There was a time when the mayoralty of New York paid more money—Governor Smith received only $10,000 a year in all years but the last of his last term, when the pay was raised to $25,000, the same figure Hylan and Walker, New York City's Mayors during the Smith regime in Albany, had been getting. The Governor, in addition, occupies the executive mansion rent-free—though some lesser persons would require coaxing to live in its somewhat gloomy atmosphere—plus servant hire, food, entertainment allowances, and travel moneys, increased in amount until they now total close to $50,000 a year above the salary itself. Mayors of New York City in recent years have had a mansion too, Gracie Mansion, with a smaller servant staff and a maintenance allowance of about $25,000.

It is a matter of record, however, that no governor has ever accumulated money in the job. The expenses of running the mansion are considerable, and Herbert H. Lehman reached frequently into his own ample pocketbook to make ends meet. Dewey, without a private fortune, increased the executive mansion household allowance in his first budget.

The functions of the Governor relating to lawmaking are dealt with in the chapter on the state Legislature. Both in this and in general, the real task of the Governor is to set policies that affect all of the citizens of the state and to handle administratively those matters too broad in scope for the cities and too localized in character for the federal government.

The state department heads who serve under him must and do bring their policy problems to the Governor, since his is the ultimate responsibility, but the day-to-day routine is something he can escape, under the structure of the state governmental machine. By his control of the purse-strings he has a check on the workings of even the few state departments whose chiefs he does not have the power to appoint, but this is exercised in connection with policy, or on occasion in connection with patronage.

Al Smith, one of the state's best administrators, found it possible to spend considerable time on his native sidewalks rather than at his desk in the Capitol. For him, the detail required less than a full work week. Roosevelt, never a first-class administrator, took the detail work lightly. Lehman, conscientious almost to a fault, was an exception, working hard at times to find work, and eschewing long vacations. Dewey has chosen to make an afternoon and evening job of it, relaxing in the mornings.

There are nineteen departments in the state government. One is headed directly by the Governor, two by other elected state officials, one by a board over which the Governor has no apparent but some actual control, and two others by boards that he can influence, leaving fourteen to be run by direct appointees of the state's chief executive.

The scope of state executive authority can best be outlined by listing the state departments and describing their functions, as briefly as possible. Omitting for a moment the Executive Department, which the Governor himself heads, they are:

Audit and Control—headed by the elected State Comptroller. It audits state and municipal accounts, sells state bonds, runs the pension system for state and local employees, and advises on state financial policies.

Taxation and Finance—headed by a commissioner and a commission, appointed by the Governor. It collects the state's taxes, estimates revenues, and runs the Motor Vehicle Bureau.

Law—headed by the elected Attorney General. It is the law office of the state government, defending it in lawsuits, and also prosecutes violations of the election, conservation, insurance, and stock frauds laws, among others.

State—headed by a secretary appointed by the Governor.

It is the general recording office of the state, for election papers, licenses, incorporations, and so on, just like a county clerk's. For reasons vaguely connected with licensing, it has under its wing three independent commissions, appointed by the Governor, which regulate boxing and wrestling, thoroughbred racing, and harness racing.

Public Works—headed by a commissioner appointed by the Governor. The department does the engineering and architectural work for state buildings and road construction, and is in charge of the maintenance of most state buildings.

Conservation—headed by a commissioner appointed by the Governor. It administers, though the Legislature frames, the rules for hunting and fishing. Under the department the State Council of Parks and individual state park commissions do the real job of running the vast state park system.

Agriculture and Markets—headed by a commissioner appointed by the Governor. It licenses stallions, bulls, and dairymen, grades farm products, pays bounties for destruction of diseased bovines, and in co-operation with the federal government administers the milk marketing orders that fix milk prices.

Labor—headed by an industrial commissioner appointed by the Governor. It is the largest department concerned with administration and policy-making and is chock-full of headaches and detail work. Under it are a group of independent or semi-independent boards and commissioners, handling workmen's compensation payments for industrial injuries; labor relations and labor mediation; minimum wages in private industry and prevailing wage scales on public works, etc. The department handles unemployment insurance and job placements directly.

Education—headed by a commissioner appointed by the Board of Regents, who are nine prominent citizens serving without salaries, elected by the Legislature. The Governor's control is only through the purse-strings or party leadership. The Regents have the power to make rules with the effect of law in the field of licensing doctors, lawyers, dentists, pharmacists, etc., plus regulation of elementary and high schools and colleges in the state and their teaching bodies. All this is done through divisions of the University of the State of New York, a unique fictional institution with no faculty, no student body, and no halls of learning.

Health—headed by a commissioner appointed by the Governor. It lays down general health policies for the state, does experimental work, regularly has charge of all local health authorities except in New York City, and can step in anywhere with broad control powers in case of emergency.

Mental Hygiene—headed by a commissioner appointed by the Governor. It is the biggest, nastiest detail job in the state. The department plays nursemaid to the state's mentally ill, a population that varies between 90,000 and 100,-000, housed in eighteen state hospitals for defectives, epileptics, and the noncriminal insane.

Corrections—headed by a commissioner appointed by the Governor. The department is the state's prison-keeper, in charge of the inmates and staffs of six state prisons, two reformatories, one vocational institution, three homes for delinquent defectives, and two hospitals for the criminal insane.

Social Welfare—headed by a commissioner appointed by an unsalaried State Board of Social Welfare, which is itself appointed by the Governor. It lays down policies for and has general supervision over all public institutions and all charity work done with the aid of state funds, including home-relief work carried on by cities.

Public Service—headed by a chairman and a commission appointed by the Governor. Its job is regulating the rates and financial operations of public-utility corporations—

keeping rates as low and bookkeeping as honest as possible —and also seeing that they furnish adequate service.

Banking—headed by a commissioner and a board all appointed by the Governor. It has supervisory power over bank operations and broad control over state bank policies.

Insurance—headed by a commissioner named by the Governor. It supervises the workings of the insurance business in the state, an undertaking of importance because the federal government does not function in this field.

Civil Service—headed by a commission appointed by the Governor. It makes the rules to carry out civil-service law requirements and holds examinations for posts that must be filled by competition.

Commerce—headed by a commissioner appointed by the Governor. It is the newest and smallest state department. Its job is advertising and promotion of state industries, resorts, and general attractions.

The Governor's own Executive Department is a hodge-podge, almost necessarily so. It takes a constitutional amendment to increase the number of state departments—Commerce was the only one added in more than twenty years—and when new state functions are assumed, their administration is often placed, as a short cut, in the Executive Department. That department quite properly contains the division of the budget, the state police and the parole board, three agencies closely tied in with the chief executive himself, and also the division of military and naval affairs, as the Governor is commander-in-chief of the state's militia. But it was only for reasons of constitutional evasion, or politics, that the business of administering liquor control, through the State Liquor Authority, was put under the Executive Department when the dry-law regime ended in 1933. The same is true of the division of housing created in 1939, which can loan state funds to subsidize low-rent housing; and that is also true of the state's commission on discrimination in employment, the state's version of a Fair Employment Practices Commission.

There are about six months a year when the Governor can relax, providing his department heads are any good, and there are another six months when he must work hard. The work really starts in the winter, directly preceding the opening of the legislative session in January. Then the Governor must map his spending program for the year, as contained in his budget, and all the policies that will lead to future state expenses and activities. During the session he must be in frequent conferences with the legislators of his own party, to drive for the enactment of his program. He must also confer with all of the leaders of the Legislature, including those of the opposite party. There will always be a dozen proposals, emanating from the Legislature, the department heads, or the citizenry, for the spending of every dollar the state has, and many of the conflicting needs will be pressing. The Governor decides. While the Legislature can refuse to spend money he has asked for, it can spend nothing without his approval, in practice if not in theory.

It is the Governor's decision, in the main, whether state employees get a pay raise; whether the allowance to localities for education is increased or decreased; whether the state continues or eliminates a child-care program; whether the need for new roads for motorists is greater than for the new hospitals they may populate; whether minimum-wage standards are enforced by the hiring of sufficient inspectors or allowed to lapse into desuetude.

During the ninety to one hundred and twenty-five days of the normal legislative session, changes in laws can be made, and money voted; so the heat is on from all quarters for policy decisions by the Governor. And after the session there is a thirty-day period of the most intense work. Under the Constitution, any bill passed before the last ten days of the session must be signed or vetoed by the Governor in ten days. The Governor may take thirty days to make up his mind on any bill passed in the last ten days. Most bills fall into the latter category, for two reasons. One is that the Legislature is naturally as dilatory as most lawmaking groups and stalls during the early part of a session, then embarks on a mad rush before adjournment. The second is that the Governor frequently requests that bills be held up so that he can act after the legislators have gone home. Whatever the reason, the executive usually has close to a thousand measures he must sign or veto in the thirty-day period. If the Governor fails to sign or veto a bill in the ten-day category, it becomes law regardless; but failure to sign in the thirty-day period acts as a veto. In practice this pocket veto is not used.

Once the thirty-day period for signing or vetoing bills is out of the way, the Governor can be relatively footloose and lighthearted for months to come. He may take a vacation, he may even take time out to campaign for the Presidency. He will spend time on patronage matters and party leadership and the problem of law enforcement.

The Governor has the power to remove or suspend incompetent or corrupt public officials, even elected ones. All Governors have used this removal power carefully and there is no recent record of abuse. The Governor also has the power to supersede local prosecuting officials in the handling of some particular case in which the Governor has grounds for feeling that the crime or scandal cannot be dealt with by the District Attorney elected for that purpose. Sometimes a District Attorney asks to be superseded for reasons that do not reflect on his integrity; sometimes the Governor steps in if it appears that a local political machine may be able to "fix" a case. Dewey's own career really started with an appointment from Governor Lehman as special prosecutor to supersede a Tammany District Attorney.

It was the practice in Lehman's time, and of the Governors preceding him, for the Governor to appoint a Democrat as a special prosecutor in territory where Republican scandals might be unearthed, and a Republican where the Democrats were in political control, to avoid the appearance or possibility of a whitewash. Dewey, who has named many special prosecutors, has, unfortunately, an unbroken record of appointing only men of his own party, regardless of whose political linen is to be washed. On more than one occasion this has led to at least the appearance of suppression of facts rather than exposure of corrupt conditions.

The Governor's office in Albany occupies most of the second floor of the vast and ugly State Capitol. Under the Dewey regime the dreary suites his predecessors had had to put up with were expanded, modernized, and redecorated. The secretariat was increased to the point where there are secretaries for the secretaries of secretaries. There was also a needed increase in the office of the counsel to the Governor, a key spot in the state governmental structure. Over the desk of the counsel there passes, at some stage of its solution, almost every state problem. Nathan R. Sobel as counsel to Lehman was contact man with the Legislature as well. Charles D. Breitel, under Dewey, runs a full-size law office in able fashion.

The secretary to the Governor has the right to sign his own name and title to a number of state papers and thus is able to take much administrative work off the Governor's hands. In the pre-Dewey days the secretary also handled press relations, but Dewey made this a separate job, giving it to the exceedingly competent James C. Hagerty under the title of Executive Assistant to the Governor. Hagerty is the son of James A. Hagerty, *Times* political reporter, and had Albany experience himself as a newspaperman. Dewey thus recognized the importance of press relations in the state government. In Albany, even before Dewey's own efforts to secure this result, the Executive Office was the chief source of news about the state government, to a greater extent than the President's staff in Washington, or the Mayor's office in City Hall, for news within their respective provinces. While departments can formulate and sometimes announce policies, their decisions become important only when approved by the chief executive.

The Governor's office has both the responsibility and the opportunity for leadership in the discussion of pending issues, and it is with the importance of that in mind, rather than from any personal bias, that the Dewey press-relations system must be criticized. Mechanically, from the point of view of convenience for working newspapermen in Albany, it is almost perfect. Press releases, or handouts, are invariably timed and given out with regard to the time of going to press of the various papers in the state and their possible interest in any particular announcement. There has been no favoritism in the handing out of news. But this concerns *handouts*. In opportunity for intelligent and critical analysis of state problems, the Dewey system represents a long step backwards. The policy has consistently been to channel any discussion of state affairs along lines directed invisibly by the Governor.

Dewey's difficulties in dealing with the press—his attempts to restrict knowledge of state affairs to what he gives out—stems from his own background, from the fact that in his first really important post as rackets prosecutor he was the sole source of news, and his statements could not be checked elsewhere. He had a hand-picked staff of assistants, and the policemen assigned to do the rough work knew they would wind up pounding pavements in the upper Bronx if they talked to the press. Secrecy was needed in the rackets probe, and the orders Dewey gave demanding it were entirely proper. His success in obtaining it was made all the greater by the fact that the people he was prosecuting, members of the underworld, were not in a position to contradict anything he gave out. Dewey found he was not only the prime source of news, but the only source. The newspapers could not check, but had to print without question, what he gave out.

Dewey was spoiled by the time he went to Albany as Governor. He was not used to being covered by men with access to additional information. It was a shock to him when reporters, instead of simply printing his announcement that he planned to save the state $25,000 by having a simple inauguration ceremony, reported also that the entire appropriation for the inaugural, in the budget, was $5,000.

After many similar incidents he worked steadily to shut down other sources of news in Albany. The objection to the funneling of information through the Governor is not very serious except for one thing: Dewey insisted, no matter how often newsmen protested, that the information he supplied be taken on faith and the fact that he was its source be undisclosed to the public.

I do not believe that a public figure—mayor, governor, or president, or even a lesser light—should be quoted on everything he says in a press conference. That would put the executive too much on guard, make him more concerned over the form of his words than the context. Neither do I question the right of a public official to deny a report —even though it is true—embodying information he is not ready to announce. Without that privilege the official would be forced into the position of having to announce many government plans when premature revelation might interfere with the desired result. Roosevelt frequently made such denials, as President and as Governor. Lehman contented himself with a blanket "no comment."

But Dewey once tried to lay down the rule that a reporter who had asked the Governor a question at a press conference could not report even that the question had been asked if the Governor did not want to answer it. The correspondents rebelled, and after a two-hour battle Dewey beat a retreat. He had since achieved something of his aim by holding few on-the-record press conferences. He held none during the time the 1947 Legislature was in session. This smacks too much of censorship, of benefit only to the incumbent, not to the public.

There was a time when the contents of the Governor's budget and of his annual message to the Legislature were kept as closely guarded secrets right up to the time that printed copies of those documents were given in confidence to the members of the press. This was during periods when there were Democratic Governors and Republican Legislatures—when disclosure of the Governor's plans might have permitted the opposition to beat the executive to the political punch. Dewey, with a Legislature controlled by his own party, and himself the leader of that party, has had no such worry about minority action, and he reversed that procedure completely. In the period immediately preceding the legislative session the Governor discloses in installments the contents and aims of his budget and his annual message, each installment covering a different phase. The papers thus print a series of stories, instead of reporting the messages on only one day, as they would otherwise do. It gives the press and the public a better opportunity to scan the coming bill of fare.

The unfortunate part of this procedure is that the press conferences at which this information is leaked out are all "off the record," and questioning the Governor's facts or motives becomes impossible. Obviously, the picture can be presented only from the point of view of the anonymous news source, and the picture at times is one-sided.

The Man in the Mansion

One executive responsibility on which the press spotlight seldom focuses, and one for which the Governor is not to be envied, is the requirement that he must stay on hand in the mansion, and the Sing Sing warden must check with him personally, on the night of the execution of a criminal. The Governor stands a death watch right up to the moment the current is turned on in the electric chair. His is the only power that can stay the hand at the switch, by granting a last-minute reprieve.

I have never discussed the question with Roosevelt or Dewey, but I do know that Lehman suffered intensely under the strain. Poletti, Governor for a month, had been familiar for years with the routine as boarder at the mansion during the Lehman regime, when he was counsel and Lieutenant Governor. It still hit him hard.

Chapter XII

ATMOSPHERIC PRESSURE

In Washington a stink is occasionally raised over the fact that some lobbyist has sat in with a congressional committee and participated in the drafting of a bill. In Albany it is done all the time and no one gets excited about it. The politically sophisticated members of the state Legislature see no harm in it, and if not done *sub rosa,* it really isn't wrong. After all, any good lobbyist knows more about the affairs of the industry or pressure group he represents than the members of the Legislature possibly can.

When the legislators start to draft a measure to regulate or curb a particular business or labor practice, the lobbyist for the group affected announces the opposition of his clients. Sometimes, for reasons this chapter will attempt to explain, that ends the bill then and there. At others, he is told: "Sorry, but we have to pass this anyhow," and then the lobbyist sits down with the committee to make the measure as harmless as possible to his client's interests. The legislators are likely to go along with him, too, providing his reservations do not interfere with the main purpose of the measure.

The legislators know that the lobbyist is a useful appendage, as important in his own way as the press, and better informed in his own particular field. Many a lobbyist, because of his special knowledge of a problem, has saved a legislator from looking foolish. The lobbyist's job is to make friends and influence people. He is co-operative.

In return, he receives favors, one of the principal of

which is the right to eliminate from the proposed "final draft" of a measure, prior to its introduction, things that would do his client the most harm and the intended beneficiaries of the legislation the least good. In this he has to be "on the level," within the peculiar legislative definition of that phrase. He may, of course, write in a joker that the committee understands and the public does not. If it is one that the committee does not understand but discovers later, he won't be favored again.

John Gunther, on his tour of America, asked in many states who really ran affairs, who were the powers behind the government; and his answers usually differ for each locality. He made no such report for New York, and the omission was not surprising. Everybody takes a hand in running New York; lobbies and pressure groups of all varieties are effective in the government of the state and of its localities. Each one plays a part, and if sometimes one is more influential than another, it is never for long.

Represented by lobbies are such obvious groups as the big industries, the banking institutions, the civil-service groups, organized labor, and the American Legion. Their lobbyists are listened to as faithfully in New York as elsewhere. Another great influence that cannot be ignored is the Catholic Church, which has shown it can effectively veto legislation it believes detrimental, such as changes in the divorce laws, legalization of birth-control information, and, earlier, ratification of the Child Labor Amendment.

And there is the teachers' lobby, for years one of the most effective, operating as it does with the co-operation of the parent-teacher associations back home. New York State has become accustomed to a high standard of education in comparison with the rest of the country, and it takes a real crisis, an actual running out of funds in the public treasury, before public officials and legislators turn down legitimate demands made by the teachers.

The State Conference of Mayors, and the Association of Towns, for years had tremendous influence in Albany with the members of the Legislature—an influence easily understood, since the legislators come from localities and return to them at the end of the session. What the local government wants is important to them, even if they are no longer directly on its payroll.

The public-utility and railroad lobbies are both conspicuous and effective. True, they long since stopped batting their heads against the wall of public opinion in connection with measures simple enough for the public to understand; but on highly technical matters of regulation and control, possibly of equal importance to them, they can pass or kill a bill just as effectively now as they did fifty years ago.

And while it may be treason, accurate reporting requires the statement that one of the most effective lobbies in any seat of government today is the newspaper lobby. Leaving out of consideration the formal representation maintained by the publishers' associations, the fact remains that most public officials are always willing to stretch things—laws, regulations, or ethics—for the sake of the reporters who cover their activities. On too many newspapers the ability of a reporter to get things done for his paper, completely outside the coverage of news, is regarded as an asset to the paper and to the reporter.

There was a classic example of this some years ago when a large metropolitan newspaper started to build a new skyscraper to house its plant. It ran into typical municipal red tape over permits and so on. It wanted a fire hydrant removed to make space for its truck runway. A street marked for one-way traffic had to be reversed so that editions of the paper could get to Grand Central terminal a few minutes faster. Things lagged until someone discovered that the paper's City Hall reporter was of the sort who make friends while covering a beat. In the short space of a year the reporter stopped covering news and was made assistant business manager of his paper, at a salary five times what he had been getting. His paper capitalized on his ability to get through to a commissioner instead of a mere deputy, to call him by his first name instead of his title, and to get things done over the telephone instead of having to get forms typed off in triplicate.

Two other lobbies that were peculiarly effective in Albany over a period of years stood out because they operated on such different sides of the economic fence. The first was that of the New York State Federation of Labor, state branch of the AFL; and the device it used was there for all to see. Each day the members of the Legislature are furnished by their clerks with calendars of the day's bills. The labor group saw to it that the members received calendars on which the federation's stand was stamped in green ink alongside each measure. The notation read: "approved by the State Federation of Labor" or "opposed by the State Federation of Labor." Members who knew nothing about some of the bills allowed themselves to be guided by the stamp, without asking questions. No other lobby ever obtained the privilege of so marking the calendars.

The other lobby referred to was run by Mark Daly, who represented a group of business interests banded together, for representation purposes, under the title of the Associated Industries of New York State. Daly never appeared on Capitol Hill except for a public hearing during the seven years I was assigned there. He stayed in his suite at the Fort Orange Club, Albany's most swank club, and entertained at lunch and at dinner. His clients back home were so important that legislators would trek up to the club to learn who in their community was interested in a particular measure and why. No one ever questioned Daly's tactics and there never appeared to be any reason for doing so. He was a well-informed, helpful representative of big business and participated as such in private conferences of legislators and leaders, as well as in round-table meetings at which labor was represented.

There are as many kinds of lobbying and as many assortments of pressure groups as there are ways of doing business and conducting the social and economic life of the community. For everybody, consciously or otherwise, is actively or potentially a member of a pressure group, depending on when, where, and how the affairs of government touch his interests. He may be landlord or tenant, school teacher or parent, laborer or employer; the consciousness of how he and his vote will be affected if he is informed of the issues, makes him a member of a pressure group in the eyes of government, whether or not he ever signs a petition, marches on Albany or City Hall, or just stays home and cusses the powers that be.

Lobbyists, of course, are ordinarily associated in the public mind with entrenched interests and organized groups, and there is no denying that on a specific matter of importance to a group the power of that group and the ability of its lobbyist will play a part in what happens. For example, it is unlikely that any private citizen ever could have induced the Legislature to do for him what was done a few years back for the House of Morgan.

The famous banking firm had decided to incorporate and it was natural that it should seek to use the name J. P. Morgan & Co., Inc. But while the move was pending, a small businessman in Queens who had operated under that corporate name some years before, revived his own incorporation papers, by paying back taxes, making impossible the use of the name by the banking house unless it bought him out, or unless the law were changed. The Morgan firm of bankers had the right contacts, and a bill that mentioned the name of neither concern, but gave the banking group the right to duplicate the existing corporate name, went quietly through the Legislature. Only the legislative leaders knew the purpose of the bill and for whose benefit it was being passed. That was not open, honest legislating. While no one ever contended that the Morgan firm bought the favor, it was a violation of the theory that the legislators and the public are at least supposed to know what is going on.

But, at that, it was a small wrong compared with a bill that the administration of the city of New York lobbied through several years later, in the cause of "good government." The situation then was that Franklin D. Roosevelt had promised Fiorello La Guardia a commission in the army, as a brigadier general, but if La Guardia left City Hall, control of the Board of Estimate, the city's governing body, would pass to the Democratic opposition, under the system of filling vacancies specified in the city charter La Guardia himself had sponsored a few years before.

So a bill was put through the Legislature, ostensibly covering leaves of absence for military service for minor public officials up-state. The bill ran to seventy-odd pages of fine type, in the opening paragraph of which New York City officials were definitely excluded from its provisions. But on page 36, in one cleverly worded sentence covering the big city, a system was set up under which La Guardia would have named his own substitute. It was a conspiracy, participated in by the Mayor, Governor Dewey, and the three principal leaders of the Legislature, to keep the fusion administration in control in New York City. The purpose was admirable, and the methods rotten. No one, not even the members who voted for the bill, had an inkling of what was going on until, weeks after the Governor had signed the measure, his press secretary let the story out so that the public mind would be somewhat prepared for the expected events. La Guardia's commission never came through, however, the Mayor never became a general, and

205

there was a disposition to forget the fact that a trick had been played, without public discussion, knowledge, or hearing, with the stakes the political control of the greatest city in the world.

All of this may tend to give a one-sided picture of the power of the organized pressure groups and of lobbyists working on the spot. But it is not only the organized lobbies and pressure groups that influence the votes of legislators and the affairs of government. The great, scantily informed mass of the electorate is also effectively represented by governing officials with knowledge of what is an issue and what is not—what may be used against them and their party effectively if they vote "wrong." Very few public officials get more than fifty-five per cent of the vote cast in the area in which they run for office. This keeps them constantly conscious of the fact that a switch of six per cent of the voters would leave them with less than a majority in the next election. They are, oh, so careful not to offend any group or combination of groups that could shift the balance. This has its disadvantages, of course. It promotes too much listening with both ears to the ground; it encourages too many legislators to sponsor all appropriation bills but no tax bills. It also means that visible groups will get from some legislators blanket approval of their programs without sufficient consideration. But it means too that the "public" has a voice more powerful than the untrained political ear realizes.

For example, New York State had, for more than a dozen years, a "mortgage moratorium" law on its statute books. It was passed in the depression years of the early thirties to make foreclosures on home and business properties difficult if not impossible. It was one of many measures passed by the Lehman "Little New Deal" in Albany, which followed in pattern, if not in detail, the outline of the Roosevelt pro-

gram in Washington, designed to ease the effect of the financial collapse of 1929.

The only thing unique about the mortgage moratorium
law was that it had to be renewed frequently. Otherwise
the courts might have objected to a declaration by the
Legislature of a "permanent" emergency, and the only way
the law could be defended as constitutional was on the
"emergency" theory. The statute had been in effect only a
few years when the banks and other lending institutions
that held most of the mortgages began lobbying for its
demise. Yet the law was passed and repassed every couple
of years until 1947, by which time the last possible excuse
for its existence had disappeared in a highly inflated real-
estate market.

The reason it was passed every time it came up for re-
newal, despite what ordinarily would have been powerful
opposition, had been stated succinctly but privately years
before by a principal leader of the Legislature; he said:
"Let's not kid ourselves. We'll have to keep this law on the
books as long as there are more people who owe money
than who lend it." The leader in question was not a Communist nor a Socialist, nor even a Democrat. He was just a
hard-bitten conservative Republican who knew the political
facts of life.

He knew that the small home-owners and small businessmen in a number of communities in the state, such as
Queens, where there had been great real-estate borrowings
before the 1929 crash, were an effective pressure group for
continuation of the debtors' legislation. The legislators of
both political parties in these areas were pledged to reten-
tion of the measure on the statute books, and a shift by
either major party would have meant political suicide. It
would have affected seats in the Legislature and the vote for
state-wide candidates as well. This particular pressure group

was much more important, and therefore much more politically effective, than the normally powerful banks, for a period of about a decade.

The banks have money power, favor-granting ability, and prestige in the political community; they have lobbyists in every seat of governmental power, including Albany, and their power is not to be underestimated; but on an open-and-shut issue, where the public could understand what was at stake and what was being done, where political retaliation at the polls was therefore likely, the "interests" didn't have a chance.

The same logic applies to rent control. It is a safe bet that rent control of some sort will remain in effect in New York State as long as there is a drastic housing shortage, for the simple reason that there are more tenants than landlords. And the tenants do not have to march on Albany with waving banners and placards to impress the legislators with their political power. Every legislator knows that if he voted against a measure outstandingly popular in his home district, the vote would be used against him, with telling effect, in the next primary or the next election.

There was one field day for lobbyists and special-interest groups in New York State in the past decade, when the boys could operate on a legislative body that did not have to run for re-election. It was in the constitutional convention of 1938, consisting of 168 delegates, fifteen elected from the state at large, and three each from the then 51 state Senate districts. Many of the delegates had never held elective public office before, and many have not held one since. Seventeen of them were judges serving long terms on the bench. Others were important public figures, but in the twilight of their careers. Only a scattering were active, functioning members of the state Legislature, and they went around shaking their heads in amazement. For it seemed to them, and to other observers, that nearly all the delegates were themselves lobbyists, there to put into the state's basic law, if they could, some idea of their own or of their clients.

One delegate whose law practice yielded him a lucrative living as a tax attorney for banks—he boasted of one fee of a million dollars—was named chairman of the committee on taxation. The banks did not suffer from the constitutional provisions he sponsored relating to the state's right to tax them. A distinguished former judge, known for both his political and his public-utility connections, sat in state on a comfortable bench in the rear of the chamber while delegates were brought back to him one by one. The other delegates were debating the issue on the floor, but a number listened while he explained why they should not vote for state power development at Niagara Falls. He was not a delegate to the convention, but he exercised more influence than most who were. Actually, he needn't have sat in the rear of the chamber. All lobbyists seemed to have the run of the floor, even while votes were being taken or provisions debated, and the president of the convention, a kindly old gentleman, had arranged for his own office to be used for "conferences," a well-meaning gesture that lent prestige to many a malodorous scheme.

One of the least edifying sights was provided by a few of the delegates who were judges. They had thought up a proposal to excuse themselves from the payment of the state income tax and scurried around openly on the convention floor to round up votes for it. To the credit of the convention and those of the judiciary who opposed such special privilege, the exemption was not granted.

There were a large number of delegates who worked consistently for the public good, lobbying only in the sense of working hard for the enactment of such things as public housing, a broader bill of rights, and greater home rule for cities. Their activities, plus the fact that any constitution adopted by the convention had to be submitted to the people—and the people rejected three groupings out of nine—produced in the end a pretty good result, but the special-interest boys did all right, too.

The convention wrote into the state's basic law one provision that will haunt budget-makers and legislators for many years, not only in Albany but in every city of the state. They did it, not to please an industry or for a lobbyist with a little black bag, but for the civil-service workers of the state and all its municipal subdivisions. The provision simply says that any pension plan set up by the state or the localities is a contractual relationship the benefits of which may never be diminished.

Pension plans are always based on what the employee contributes plus what the employer contributes plus what their pooled investment will earn in interest. At present, pension funds that were based on an investment yield of, say, four per cent are earning much less, and the state and its localities must dig up in tax revenues constantly increasing amounts to meet the swiftly accumulating pension-fund deficits. The cities and the state may at some future date approach bankruptcy, but the grip fastened on their treasuries by that one lobby can never be broken. Even a second constitutional amendment repealing the first would be illegal, under the federal constitutional provision that prevents a state from doing anything to abrogate a contract.

Another example of a successful lobby working for a large group of people, but at the same time adversely affecting the general welfare, is a purely local one. It is generally agreed that the obsolete building codes maintained by cities constitute one of the obstacles to solving the housing problem. They prohibit the use in homes of building materials that were not in existence when the codes were drawn up and they do not permit the use of new, labor-saving methods of construction. A chief factor in keeping these codes on the books is the attitude of the building trades unions. The codes are usually the responsibility of the local board of aldermen or council. In each case the building trades either are represented directly on the local governing body, or are able to exert effective political pressure on them to maintain what I believe is a shortsighted monopoly.

Most people forget that there is just as much lobbying going on, just as much pressure-group representation, at City Hall as there is in Albany or in Washington. Lobbyists must register in Washington and in Albany, and they have to maintain headquarters or make trips by train to the Capitol. They don't in local matters. A visit to the Mayor's office attracts little attention, and a nickel telephone call to the leader of the majority in the council attracts less. But in any city hall in the state the pleas of organized groups, be they of high or low degree, receive consideration from the mayor and the council, from the department heads and from the political bosses who put them in office, or else they do not count on holding their jobs for very long.

Local political pressure is sometimes extremely important in matters far removed from the local scene. It is pressure-group action transmuted into the purest form of political pressure. For example, big city political organizations, dependent on the labor vote, made known to President Truman, in undisguised form, their demand that he veto, for their sake, the Taft-Hartley revision of the Wagner Labor Relations Act. Only a few months later, when the State Department first began wavering on pressing for adoption of the Palestine partition plan, it was Frank Hague of Jersey City and Ed Flynn of the Bronx who told the President that the Democratic party label wouldn't be worth a hoot in hell the following election in their constituencies unless the plan was implemented by American pressure.

One New York City administration was booted out of office by the resentment of women, who did not then even have the vote. It happened in the time of John Purroy Mitchel, reform Mayor of New York from 1913 to 1917. The Mitchel administration, one of the purest and best-intentioned in the city's history, reorganized the school system. In so doing, it raised hob with the standard school lunch hour. Staggered sessions were arranged for pupils before the days of school lunchrooms, and the city's mothers found that they had to prepare separate lunches for their various progeny, who returned home at different hours. The Mitchel administration made other mistakes, but that one counted heaviest, and out it went at the next election.

This chapter has not dealt with several important fields of operation of pressure groups and lobbyists. One that is little known is a "brains" lobby carried on as a volunteer duty by a number of men attracted by the problems of government and public life, yet who do not hold or even seek public office. They usually remain anonymous when called in by the executive or the legislature because of their special knowledge of special fields. They draw bills, participate in public planning, and help make public policy without pay or glory.

One who worked so long in this way, and so effectively that his activities became well known, was Charles C. Burlingham, many times president of the Association of the Bar of the City of New York, and a force for good in its activities. If ever a man came close to personifying disinterested civic virtue in New York City, it was Mr. Burlingham, who remained active even when an octogenarian. He was responsible to some extent for La Guardia's nomination for mayor, and during the entire dozen years of the La Guardia administration he acted as an inspiration to La Guardia in many ways, and also as a check on sometimes

212

ill-considered plans. La Guardia would take a dressing-down from him and from no one else in the world.

Then there are civic groups, like the League of Women Voters, the Citizens Union, and the bar associations, which frequently take stands on matters of general public concern and seek to influence executives and legislators in their handling of public problems. It is suspected by seasoned observers that government officials follow the advice of these groups only when it suits a previously decided course of action, and ignore them with impunity in other cases, for the reason that they have not shown themselves capable of exerting effective political pressure.

Finally, there is the common or garden variety of political lobbying, the favor-doing for which political organizations always have existed, on which they pride themselves, and with which the public is or should be quite familiar. Mentioning it is enough. It leads to consideration of the general ethics of "favor-doing."

Some favors are done for cash. This has always been dangerous and today is regarded as obsolete. One who gets a reputation for taking cash loses his effectiveness in places like Albany or City Hall, because his colleagues shy away from helping him, for fear he may be "selling" them as well as himself while keeping the entire proceeds. Leaving cash sales of favors aside, the fact remains that some favors are legitimate; others are not. Drawing the line where honest favors turn into abuses is almost impossible. For example, consider one of the commonest and most effective types of lobbying practiced by business these days.

An enterprise employing a large number of people in a medium-size up-state city desires a change in a section of a law that affects its business. The head of the business does not pack a brief-case with greenbacks and go to Albany to buy support. Instead he drops across the street from his office to Republican or Democratic county headquarters to see the county chairman. The chairman agrees that the law should be changed and says he will do something about it, since no one would be hurt and a local industry would be benefited. The county chairman takes his annual trip to Albany, for which he has been saving up a number of such "contracts," and he tells the leaders there—who have been using his county legislative contingent to bolster their party majorities all session—that the bill is important to him and to his community. He secures, of course, the necessary agreement on its passage.

Not a penny has been passed, not a corrupt promise made. Most persons would agree that while a back door was used, no evil entered. But suppose that the business enterprise was one that was always good for a substantial campaign contribution, and that was why the chairman took the trouble to go to Albany. Is that corruption? Does the deal become more corrupt if the company is a new one in the community and the head of it indicates he will become a substantial contributor in the future if the party can help him? Suppose the county chairman was a lawyer and the concern one of his clients—is it then corrupt or is it only corrupt if the company becomes a client and gives up a substantial fee after the granting of the favor?

Suppose one of the legislative leaders is in the insurance business. A direct approach is made to him for a legitimate favor. He grants it and, lo, the company, out of gratitude, transfers its insurance business to him as agent. Corruption? The line is a hard one to draw, and if it can be drawn at all, that must be done in the minds of the participants in the deal. It is probable that more often than not governmental favors are handed out on a basis of you scratch my back and I'll scratch yours.

It may be wrong, but until everybody, in some future utopia, treats everybody else with equal abstract justice,

214

favors will be done for pressure groups, for lobbyists, and for businessmen who can return them. Politicians regard the principle as no different from that involved when the clerk gets his brother a job as office boy, the landlord evicts a tenant to rent his vacant apartment to a relative, and a wholesaler sells at retail to his daughter's roommate at college.

Chapter XIII

THE CITIES AND THE STATE

Most laymen will confess that they do not know where the power of the state ends and that of the city begins. The truth is that there is no exact line. The cities, the Legislature, and the courts have been trying for years to establish some fixed boundary of governmental controls and have not succeeded.

If one starts from the premise that the cities have no basic power, not even the right to exist except by state permission, one begins to get the picture. The cities of New York—and there are sixty-two of them—are all creatures of the state. The states themselves created and gave power to the federal government, but the cities did not form the states. When the nation was formed, the states already had their governmental power, and over the years they have chartered cities within their borders as municipal corporations, just as they have chartered private corporations.

Under those charters cities have the power, freely given to them by the state, to do all the nasty municipal household chores, and, if the analogy may be carried farther, the state steps in only when the housewife goes over her budget, or when company is present. For other things the state sometimes gives rights and sometimes takes them away again.

The best example of how a state can grant power and then retract it came up in connection with some New York

216

The Cities and the State

City local taxes a few years ago. The city was broke when La Guardia took office as Mayor, and the Legislature gave the city administration the authority to cut some municipal salaries and also to adopt some new taxes other than taxes on real estate. It left to the city the choice of the taxes to be imposed.

La Guardia then did the impossible. He devised not one, but three successful taxes—the sales tax, the cigarette tax, and the public-utility tax—all successful in the sense that the public paid them without squawking too loudly and the pennies collected rolled up into hundreds of millions of dollars of needed city revenues.

A few years later the state itself was in a bad need of additional revenues, and Herbert H. Lehman, as Governor, with the consent of the Legislature, moved into the utility-tax field. La Guardia could do nothing about it. The next year the Legislature, rejecting an income-tax increase proposed by Lehman, took over the cigarette tax for the state, too. There was sentiment for assumption of the sales tax as well, but up-state opposition defeated this. The opposition was not on the ground that New York City had developed this particular revenue, which it needed so badly, and was therefore entitled to keep it. It was based on a fear of loss of business by localities bordering on Pennsylvania and Canada if a state-wide sales tax were imposed.

In none of these cases did the state seize the revenues collected by the city—it just took over the source on a state-wide basis. The city was allowed to impose a utility tax of its own if it desired, and for a short period it was allowed to pyramid the tax on cigarettes, too. That eventually brought a protest from the citizenry, so the *city's* cigarette tax was abolished.

In New York State, as in most states, the basic revenues of cities are derived from taxation of real estate, within limits imposed by the state Constitution. The state, which

217

once had a realty tax of its own, gave that up about twenty years ago in favor of taxes on income and business, motor vehicles, and later liquor and racing. In recent years the cities generally have needed more revenues than the realty tax afforded within the constitutional limits, so the Legislature, under the Dewey administration, gave them a continuing right to levy additional taxes. The state having already pre-empted the field of profitable and relatively painless taxation, the localities have been left with those in the nuisance category and most cities have hesitated to impose them.

On the other hand, the state is not just a money-grubbing miser. It returns to the cities, the towns, and the villages a major portion of its revenues by contributing to education costs—on a varying formula designed to secure an even level of education throughout the state—and it pays back to the localities a share of what they have to spend on welfare activities, to list two major contributions. The state's share of home-relief costs is eighty per cent at this writing.

The state gives out money for road construction as well, and in all three fields, it may be noted, the state receives aid from the federal government, which it passes on. But most of these allocations, and even local sharing of state-collected taxes on a percentage basis, were made on haphazardly for years. Percentages were completely unscientific, based purely on what trading had to be done at some particular past point in history to squeeze the tax or aid program through the Legislature. For example, the localities always retained a percentage of the corporate-franchise tax—the state income tax on corporations—paid by those companies with home offices in the locality. During the recent war this turned into a real bonanza for up-state villages that suddenly became the sites of new war industries. They received far more than it was ever intended they should have—so much more than they needed that the law was changed. But meanwhile many a long-standing bonded debt was paid off.

It is impossible for every locality to receive as much in the form of state aid as its inhabitants pay to the state in taxes, or more. Obviously, if it did, the state would have nothing left for operating its own machinery. So despite all attempts to devise a permanent scientific formula for contributions by the state, or sharing of state revenues, the real criterion has remained need. The state gives back to the localities what they need to carry on, beyond what they themselves can raise, within the limits of what is deemed politically advisable at the time. Explanations that sound higher-minded may be given, but need plus politics remains the standard.

Emphasis has been placed thus far on the money question. It is important. But there is another aspect of the city-state relationship just as important and much more complicated. It involves how much "home rule" the cities are, or should be, allowed—how much they may govern themselves. In some states the legislatures really run the cities at will —Massachusetts solons are always openly engaged in running the city of Boston—but in New York State there is a greater appearance of local autonomy.

Technically, the cities of New York have home rule to the extent of control over their own "property, affairs and government." They also have the right to adopt laws with purely local effect, providing that these laws are not inconsistent with the state laws or Constitution, and the Legislature, in turn, is prohibited from passing laws affecting only a single city, or several cities, except when asked for such action. This grant of local power and autonomy sounds like much more than it really is.

In the first place, the city's right to legislate in a manner not "inconsistent" with state law means that any time the city passes a law the state does not like, the state can make that law "inconsistent" by passing a state law in the same field.

In addition, no legislature and no constitutional convention in New York has ever been willing to give up the state's right to step into city affairs in an emergency, or the power to legislate in general terms for all cities. Quite possibly the state should never give up this power; it may be that the localities can not be trusted completely, and state power must be reserved. But in practice, because the state has kept this "reserve" power, it has consistently used it, whether there is an emergency or not, with or without the consent or connivance of the localities.

At my request, Reuben A. Lazarus, for many years New York City's representative in Albany, and generally regarded as the leading expert on home-rule questions, briefly outlined the history and present status of home-rule powers. According to Mr. Lazarus, the fight for home rule began about one hundred years ago and the first grant of power came when a provision was written into the state Constitution of 1894 requiring the Legislature to submit all bills that affected fewer than all the cities of the state to the mayors of those cities. A mayor had fifteen days to consider the measure. If he vetoed the bill as it applied to his city, the Legislature could override the veto by a simple majority vote. If he approved, the bill became law. Since most bills were passed then, as now, in the last ten days of sessions, such vetoes were practically conclusive.

But the cities kept demanding affirmative legislative power as well as the veto power, and they finally got it in 1923 by a constitutional amendment prepared by a Home Rule Commission. The amendment gave the cities the right to act on their own "property, affairs and government," but reserved to the Legislature the right to pass general laws in any field. Also, special laws affecting only one city could be passed by a two-thirds vote after a special request from the Governor.

Mr. Lazarus believes that the Legislature that adopted the Home Rule Amendment of 1923 did so grudgingly, and deliberately kept the phrasing as vague as possible. In any event, after various interpretations by the courts, the net result was that the state retained the right to step in, almost at will, on the excuse that the lives, health, or safety of the citizenry were somehow involved. As local an affair as regulating building construction became a state, not a city right under one notable court decision.

In addition—and at this point I am not quoting Mr. Lazarus—the cities developed the habit of running to Albany to have their local legislation passed there by a two-thirds vote. Sometimes this was done to forestall legal questions; at others it was done as a buck-passing device.

For example, a large number of city salaries and wage scales are now mandatory by state law. Often when city employees went to a mayor for a pay raise, he told them he'd like to give it to them, but feared opposition from the local taxpayers. He suggested that they get a bill passed at Albany, where local opposition would be less effective. They followed his advice, the pay raise became law, and the mayor requested the funds for it in his next budget as an expenditure from which there was no escape. He even grumbled and groaned about encroachment on his power.

At the constitutional convention of 1938 there was a long and bitter battle over extension of home rule. The state's "reserve" power was the crux of it. One change provided that requests for the passage of a bill of local effect by a two-thirds vote of the Legislature must come from the administration of the city affected, rather than from the Governor. At the same time the Legislature's right to adopt laws of local effect relating to matters other than "property, affairs and government" by a simple majority was vigorously reaffirmed.

In Mr. Lazarus's opinion, the power of the cities was not really enlarged by the 1938 amendment; only the language was clarified.

One must not get the idea that there is a consistent record of abuse of the localities by the state because the latter's control is so complete. In practice the cities have a powerful lobby in Albany, and the legislators listen to what their home-town mayors have to say, particularly if the mayors have support from the local political organization.

In addition, the mayors are in communication with the Governor's office on matters affecting their particular localities, and it is customary for the Governor to ask the mayor of a city for a memorandum on any bill passed that affects his city. Even if the Governor should neglect to do this, it would be perfectly in order for the mayor to send a memorandum. In nearly all cases where broad aspects of state policy are not involved and there is no important political pressure on the Governor urging an opposite course, the mayor's recommendation concerning a particular bill is accepted. Often the Governor incorporates the mayor's opinion in his own final message of veto or approval.

No governor would enjoy running for re-election in a locality that had been convinced that under his administration of the state it had suffered grievous wrongs. Nor could he expect consistent legislative support for measures that convinced all the urban residents of the state that they were being discriminated against.

As noted in the chapter on the Legislature, the situation of the Republican Party in the state as a whole improved considerably when the up-state GOP leaders in that body stopped opposing New York City legislative requests simply because of the source.

In the 1947 municipal elections in the state the Republicans suffered losses of council seats and other local offices in Buffalo and Syracuse because the local administrations imposed new taxes, authorized by the Dewey state administration, while the state itself continued to pile up a surplus. The people there felt they were being bilked, that they should have received help instead of new burdens sanctioned by the state. And the fact that the municipal aid formula had been revised "scientifically" only two years before did not assuage their pocketbook pains.

One power that the state has over the cities no one questions. It is the one designed to check and expose municipal corruption. Under that power the Governor may remove any or all elected local officials, on charges, after a hearing. The Governor is the sole judge of the sufficiency of the evidence. In Franklin D. Roosevelt's famous removal of Sheriff Thomas (Tin-Box Tom) Farley of New York County, the Governor laid down a new rule—and it was not challenged—that a public official was obliged to give the public a reasonable explanation of money he had amassed during his term of office.

Still another refinement written into the state Constitution in 1938 requires public officials to waive immunity before any grand jury investigating the affairs of their office, or else forfeit that office. And there always remains in the background the right of the Legislature to appoint a committee with the broadest of powers to investigate the affairs of any city, any locality, and any of its officers.

The most famous investigation of this kind was that conducted by the Hofstadter legislative committee. It was better known as the Seabury investigation, after the counsel who dominated the committee's course of action. It was the Seabury investigation that caused the removal of Sheriff Farley and the resignation of Mayor Jimmy Walker of New York City while he was under removal charges before the Governor.

One of the best-kept secrets of that era concerns a prominent up-state Republican who had served in the Legislature with Jimmy and was very fond of him. The Republican in question still had much to say about how the Legislature was run. He went to Walker before the probe was voted for and told him that party strategy called for the investigation of New York City affairs, but if it might show Jimmy to have done anything wrong, it could still be stopped. It was a case of friendship coming ahead of party or government. Walker, proud to the last, told his friend that no investigation would ever "get anything on me"; the friend accepted his assurances. The rest is history.

Chapter XIV

WHO'S GOING TO WIN?

The Constitution and the election law in New York State both contain provisions barring from voting any person who has made a bet on the result of an election. The ban was written in many years ago, not to discourage gambling per se, but to prevent evasion of companion sections that prohibit the buying of votes for cash. Without that bar to betting, those interested in buying votes would have lost a large number of two- and five-dollar bets that they never expected to win anyway.

As it stands, the law prohibiting betting on elections is obsolete and unenforced, and operates only to prevent people in high political position, such as candidates themselves, from disclosing that they had bet on the result. The people as a whole do a lot of friendly wagering, and there is much more done, in an attempt to make money, with the bookies along Broadway.

It is a tribute to the simplicity of motivation of the bookmaking fraternity—concerned only with paying out less than they take in—that the bookie odds have practically always reflected the winning candidate. I do not recall a single instance in a major race—barring the Wilson-Hughes freak election of 1916—when the man they made the favorite has not won the election. This is so well recognized by professional politicians that they have frequently considered spending a few thousand dollars to bring down the odds and thus prevent a rush to the favorite—and opposition—candidate, by bandwagon voters. Sometimes they have even attempted it.

The bookies are not guided by sentiment or agreement with a candidate's views on either domestic or international questions. They always keep in mind that only one man can win, and once they have decided which candidate that is, the odds they give are immaterial except for the few who like to maintain what they call at the track a "balanced book." The bookies know that there is really no such thing as a two-to-one bet on an election, and that three-, four-, or five-to-one bets are simply evidence that wise men are taking advantage of suckers. It is scant comfort afterwards to know that you lost at five-to-one while your friend got only a four-to-one chance on the same fool bet.

If the bettor is acting on information and judgment, he can offer ten to one, and still receive a higher return on his money than American Telephone & Telegraph stock will yield. If the race is so extremely close that he does not *know* who is going to win, he should neither give nor take less than even money.

Apart from the bookies, who issue no claims and are just as happy being ignored except by clients, many pretensions of infallibility in predicting election results have been made by various polls. Most of these claims are unfounded and are justified only by amendatory and explanatory statements made after the election is over and the votes have been counted. This is particularly true of predictions concerning New York elections.

The most famous flop of all time was the *Literary Digest* poll of 1936, which predicted the election of Alf M. Landon as president. He carried only Maine and Vermont. The *Digest* poll showed Landon would carry New York, and he lost it by more than a million votes. Yet the *Digest* poll was potentially the best of them all. It attempted to get a response from a larger cross-section of the electorate than any

other, and, the bigger the cross-section, the greater the
chance of inaccuracies canceling themselves out. The *Digest*
sent postcards to ten per cent of the electorate to be returned unsigned. There was no exact check on who turned
in which ballot, although the area from which the card
came could be identified.

There was a major opportunity for error in the *Digest*
system in that it relied too much on the telephone book and
not enough on the lists of registered voters. Thus it hit a
higher economic stratum—people who could afford tele-
phones—than the average of the nation. Despite this, the
Digest poll was accurate enough to pick the winners in the
national election of 1932 and in the New York City three-
cornered mayoralty election of 1933. But in 1936, while no
one ever accused the *Digest* of miscounting the ballots it
received, there was ample evidence to justify a conclusion
that the magazine was seeking a result rather than reporting one. In New York, where the announced result of the
poll gave the state to Landon, separate subsidiary reports
put out by the magazine showed clearly that it had sent out
twice as many ballots to up-state Republican territory as it
had to Democratic New York City, and by adding the results established a Republican percentage majority, which
it then multiplied by ten, as the *Digest* ten per cent rule
justified.

It happened that this was in defiance of the most elementary rule of political computation, which is that in any
state where there is an up-state, down-state political division, the percentages must be figured separately and then,
and only then, projected into a state-wide result. The
Digest's own figures, if separated into the proper up-state,
down-state divisions and computed on the percentage of
the vote to be cast in each area, clearly showed the state
would go to Roosevelt.

The *Digest* also predicted that Pennsylvania would go

Republican, but again the subsidiary reports, covering the cities, showed Pittsburgh and Philadelphia both would be carried by Roosevelt, and the Pennsylvania situation was such that if both those cities went Democratic, so would the state as a whole.

Acting solely on the digested *Digest* information, I won several small bets that year that Pennsylvania would go Democratic. It did, for the first time since the Civil War.

The most prominent poll since the *Digest* gave up the ghost has been the Gallup poll, which is a "sampling" device. It is widely quoted, and on the basis of the reliance placed on it by many thousands of persons in and out of politics, the supposition would be that it has a long record of having accurately predicted election results. It happens that in neither of the last two key elections, 1940 and 1944, did the Gallup poll predict the re-election of President Roosevelt.

In 1940 it made no prediction at all. In 1944, after leaving the result in doubt up to a week before election, it came out the day before election giving Roosevelt the edge, but by a percentage majority of the popular vote that the proprietor of the poll had consistently warned was insufficient for the election of a Democratic nominee. It left in doubt enough of the key states to permit Dewey to win, and made no prediction at all on Roosevelt's probable total electoral vote. This was the Gallup poll record for the nation in 1940, when the electoral total was 449 for Roosevelt and 82 for Willkie, and in 1944, when the totals were 432 for Roosevelt and 99 for Dewey.

The Gallup system seems to be designed to avoid an outright prediction of the election result, but to bury down deep enough data to support the correct conclusion. The sponsor later points to this with pride.

So far as predicting the result in New York State was concerned, in the 1940 election it first put Roosevelt in the lead, and then Willkie, by a 51 to 49 per cent margin, another figure that the sponsor of the poll has said meant nothing because it did not cover the 3 per cent margin of error he allowed himself. In 1944 the poll, even on the final day, gave New York State to Dewey by a narrow margin, with the only doubtful element being the soldier vote, which had not been canvassed. There was some reason for considering New York State doubtful in 1940, as there was no real way at that time of knowing how the shadow of impending World War II would affect the electorate, up-state in particular. But in 1944 putting New York State in the Dewey column represented either gross inaccuracy or wishful thinking.

One other poll, the Dunn survey, also using a sampling process, predicted the election of Landon in 1936, then told its subscribers afterward that it had been wrong because it failed to take into account the WPA vote. Four years later it predicted the election of Willkie and explained after election that it had erred because it forgot to weigh in the vote of government employees. Even if both these explanations are accepted as genuine, they still show how a small degree of error in a narrow sampling can be capitalized into a completely fallacious "result."

It should be explained what a sampling is. Under a sampling, the people running the poll never make public the number of people interviewed; they simply give percentage results on guinea-pig voters. These percentages are not actual, but weighted, in the light of the knowledge or supposed knowledge of those running the polls as to what percentage of the electorate fits into the same category as those who have actually been interviewed. Gallup, called before a congressional committee after the 1944 election to explain his errors, admitted that he had cut down the

229

Roosevelt percentages because he had figured on a small vote being cast in the nation as a whole and regarded this as favorable to Dewey.

On the other hand, the polls have shown at times that they can be accurate. The *Fortune* Roper poll, while less known than Gallup's, seems to come close to the actual result with reasonable consistency. And in the very close New York State election of 1938, when Lehman beat Dewey by 64,000 votes, the Gallup poll gave Lehman 50.2 per cent of the vote and he actually received 50.7. That result did more to make the reputation of the Gallup poll than any other one thing.

The *New York Daily News,* which conducts a house-to-house survey around New York State prior to state and national elections, was as right in its percentages in 1938 as the Gallup poll, but it gave the election to Dewey by a few thousand votes. Even though the *News* picked the wrong candidate as the winner, it was nearer in percentages than it has ever been since.

In elections since 1938, and increasingly so each year, the *News* poll has produced results heavily weighted in favor of whichever candidate or party it happened to be supporting editorially. No accusation of ill faith on the part of the *News* is intended. It is probable that there is a small percentage of the population, called upon by a *News* canvasser to cast what amounts to an open ballot, that will tell the canvassers what it thinks the paper wants to know while concealing its true voting intentions. Since the *News* poll, while making a sampling far larger than that attempted by Gallup or anyone else, is limited to one per cent of the enrolled voters, any error would be greatly multiplied in the final computation. Whatever the cause, the *News* poll reached such a state of inaccuracy in 1946 that it gave Dewey twice the majority he received on election day. That was close to 700,000 and needed no magnifying.

Who's Going to Win?

The *News*, apart from its close but wrong guess in 1938, has never picked the wrong man as the winner; it has simply been far off on its predicted majorities. This does have the effect, unintentional as it may be, of increasing the majority of the winning candidate over what it otherwise would have been. For a poll to indicate that candidate A will win by a million votes over candidate B has a definite and deleterious effect on the campaign of candidate B. His supporters lose heart, contributions are held up, some voters stay away from the polls, loath to waste time supporting a hopeless cause. Voters without definite convictions, who have not made up their minds, vote for candidate A because he is going to win anyway.

Providing the poll is correct in picking A to win, the only effect on candidate B is to increase the margin by which he would have lost anyhow. But the effect on the running-mates of candidate B, seeking lesser office, is sometimes more serious. Suppose they might win in anything but an opposition landslide. The landslide is stimulated by the erroneous prediction of the poll, and everybody running with B loses.

There was a time when efficiently functioning party organizations in New York could predict the result state-wide or city-wide. In the 1928 election James A. Hagerty, political reporter for the *New York Times,* predicted in his newspaper that Herbert Hoover would carry the state over Al Smith for president by a margin of 110,000 votes. Hoover's majority was 111,000. Hagerty used as the basis of his prediction the confidential figures in the hands of H. Edmund Machold, then Republican state chairman. He knew, and Machold knew, that the figures were accurate. The Machold figures were based on canvasses made by a smooth-functioning machine. Similarly, in New York City, a Tammany Board of Strategy, headed by John H. Delaney and Daniel L. Ryan, using the reports of house-to-house canvasses made

231

in selected districts, often calculated percentages so close to the final result as to appear miraculous.

But with the decline in power of the machines, it is no longer possible to get figures of validity on a state- or city-wide basis. Locally, there are spots like the "southern tier" counties, where William H. Hill can call the GOP majority within a handful of votes, or Albany, where the O'Connells can do the same in the opposite party.

One "statistician" for one of the major parties in recent years, using the figures of the previous election, assumed on faith and hope that his party would do 8, 10, or 12 per cent better in the coming election and computed totals for all counties on that basis. He could make up as pretty a set of exact-looking inaccuracies as anyone could want.

To make up your own private sampling, simply talk to as many persons as possible, finding out how they voted in the preceding comparable election and how they intend to vote this time. Then ignore those who are voting under the same party emblem as before. Concentrate on those who intend to switch, since they make the difference in the totals from the previous election. Try to find out why they are switching. If you really find out why, you will have as good an idea of the result coming up as anyone.

Finding out why people change is not always simple. For example, in 1940 many persons who had voted for Roosevelt in 1936 said that they were against a third term. Many millions of words were written and spoken that year about the importance of the "third-term issue." In every case I encountered, by pressing for more than casual information I found that the voter disapproved of a majority of F. D. R.'s acts in the previous four years, making it highly probable that not one of the persons interviewed would have voted for Roosevelt in 1940 had he been running then for only a second term. Possibly some few persons in the state and nation in 1940 really preferred Roosevelt to Willkie and nevertheless voted for Willkie on the third-term issue, but I did not meet any. I did meet hundreds who used the third-term candidacy as a conversational short cut in explaining their switch.

So much for the practice of trying to name election winners through polls. In the case of the sponsored polls, the relative success achieved can be checked with election results over the years. Those that stray too far out of line will suffer the fate of the *Digest*.

But there are other samplings, conducted by groups such as the Gallup organization, which never can be checked. If Gallup or any one of his rivals says in May of a presidential year that possibility A will run better than possibility B against the incumbent C, no one can ever tell whether that declaration was right at the time it was made or whether it was entirely wrong. The same goes for any "testing" of public sentiment on military training, partition of Palestine, reaction to the Taft-Hartley law, or aspects of our foreign policy.

In connection with the possible voting strength of various candidates, it would be perfectly possible for some future rival of Dr. Gallup to set up a sampling poll, achieve a reputation for accuracy on election results, and use that reputation from then on to influence the deliberations of a convention of politicians seeking to find a sure winner in a presidential race. It would be possible for the sponsor of that poll to indicate early in a presidential year that party A was a sure winner over party B and thus lead party A to select a candidate for reasons other than proved vote-getting ability. Or it could take the opposite tack and indicate that the election would be close, or that party B had an edge, leading party A to nominate its best vote-getter. The potentialities for political influencing, rather than reporting, are enormous.

As long as the federal Constitution contains a guarantee

of freedom of the press, nothing can be done to abolish polls. But it remains true that predictions can be made long before an election for the purpose of influencing it, and later the sponsors can hedge and finally make forecasts close to the actual result, explaining with good grace that speeches by the various candidates have caused "swings in sentiment," or attributing the change to new conditions at home or abroad.

Which brings up another question. How much does a campaign influence the actual result? In the opinion of many, the countless speeches and broadcasts and the press handouts that are so familiar a part of all campaigns for high office have little if any influence that cannot be calculated in advance. Take the campaigning ability of the candidates, for example their radio voices. The difference never showed up so much as it did in 1936, when Alf Landon's Kansas twang was matched against Franklin Roosevelt's golden voice. Roosevelt's voice influenced his audiences, but everybody knew in advance that it would. In 1944 Roosevelt's greatest assets, no doubt, were the position he held as war-time commander-in-chief and the prestige of having sat down frequently with Churchill and Stalin to map out world affairs. This was known before the campaign, and the only question was that of Roosevelt's health, which he was able to answer satisfactorily—for the campaign, anyhow.

Chance incidents have sometimes affected extremely close elections. The cry of "Rum, Romanism, and Rebellion" raised against the candidates of the Democratic party by an up-state bluenose undoubtedly helped James G. Blaine lose New York State to Grover Cleveland. But so did McKane's vote-stealing in Coney Island, previously noted. In 1916 Charles Evans Hughes stayed overnight at the same hotel as Hiram Johnson, California's leading Progressive. Hughes never called on Johnson, the latter took umbrage, and the Johnson supporters knifed the ticket sufficiently to cost Hughes the state of California and the election. Hughes, according to those who knew the situation at the time, never knew Johnson was at hand, the information being kept from him by the California "stalwarts" opposed to Johnson. The latter had run for vice president with Teddy Roosevelt on the Progressive ticket in 1912; but even there the difficulties inherent in trying to patch together the Republican Party for the 1916 campaign, of which the Johnson incident was a good example, were well known before the campaign.

Usually campaign breaks are so distributed among opponents that they cancel out. In New York City in 1941 Fiorello La Guardia, running for his third term as Mayor, was expected to win by something under 150,000 votes. He was appreciably weaker than he had been in 1937, but he was "safe." As the campaign progressed, however, William O'Dwyer, the Democratic nominee, failed to make a dent in the public consciousness and a bandwagon movement to La Guardia was definitely under way. His potential majority soared upward, and La Guardia, alert to the trend, got cocky. He decided to polish off Herbert Lehman, still Governor, at the same time. For no reason at all, he started calling Lehman names, and immediately lost support from groups of voters who would normally have supported both La Guardia and Lehman. La Guardia eventually won the election by a majority of 139,000, about the same he would have had if O'Dwyer had made a good campaign.

What it adds up to is this:

The factors that lead up to the nomination of the rival candidates—their personalities and past records; their social views and the political, economic, and racial forces lined up for and against them; the methods by which they are nomi-

235

nated, including the factor of party unity or discord—pretty well settle the election before a single speech is made by the candidate. One might as well place one's bet the day after the opposing slates have been named. After that, all is noise and confusion.

A CALENDAR OF KEY ELECTIONS IN
NEW YORK STATE, 1918–1946

1918—Alfred E. Smith elected Governor the first time, defeating Charles S. Whitman.

1920—Harding-Coolidge ticket sweeps state against Democratic national ticket of James M. Cox and Franklin D. Roosevelt; Smith bows to Nathan L. Miller in the landslide.

1922—Smith elected Governor a second time, defeating Miller.

1924—Calvin Coolidge wins majority in state over both John W. Davis, Democrat, and Robert M. La Follette, Progressive, for president. Smith is only Democrat elected state-wide, defeating the late Theodore Roosevelt, Jr.

1925—James J. Walker wins New York mayoralty from Frank D. Waterman, Republican, after defeating John F. Hylan, the incumbent, for the Democratic nomination.

1926—Smith elected Governor the fourth time, defeating Ogden L. Mills, Republican.

1928—Hoover carries state for President over Smith, but Franklin D. Roosevelt is elected Governor and Herbert H. Lehman Lieutenant Governor.

1929—Walker is re-elected Mayor of New York, defeating Fiorello H. La Guardia.

1930—Roosevelt wins second term as Governor and Lehman as Lieutenant Governor, over Charles H. Tuttle and Caleb Baumes.

1932—Roosevelt carries state and nation for the Presidency, Lehman is elected Governor, and John P. O'Brien be-

237

comes Mayor for a year to fill vacancy caused by Walker's resigning.

1933—La Guardia is elected Mayor of New York for first time, in contest with O'Brien, Democrat, and Joseph V. McKee, independent.

1934—Lehman is re-elected Governor over Robert Moses, and Legislature goes Democratic.

1936—Roosevelt carries state and nation against Alf M. Landon; Lehman is elected to third term as Governor. American Labor Party appears on ballot for first time.

1937—La Guardia wins election as Mayor for second time, over Jeremiah T. Mahoney; Thomas E. Dewey elected District Attorney of New York County.

1938—Lehman wins fourth term as Governor, for new four-year term, over Dewey.

1940—Roosevelt carries state over Willkie in third-term election.

1941—La Guardia wins third election as reform Mayor of New York.

1942—Dewey is elected Governor on Republican ticket, defeating John J. Bennett, Jr., Democrat, and Dean Alfange, American Labor Party candidate.

1944—Roosevelt defeats Dewey for the Presidency in the state and nation. Liberal Party becomes a separate party.

1945—William O'Dwyer elected Mayor of New York on Democratic and American Labor tickets, against Newbold Morris, independent, and Jonah J. Goldstein, Republican-Liberal candidate.

1946—Dewey re-elected over James M. Mead, Democrat; Irving M. Ives, Republican, defeats Herbert H. Lehman for United States Senatorship.

Index

Adirondacks, 167
Agriculture Adjustment Administration, 82
Agriculture and Markets Dept., 190
"Ahearn crowd," 160
Albany, 37, 41, 42, 65, 66, 73, 77, 88, 94, 110, 115, 139–41, 158, 175, 179–81, 188, 195–7, 200, 203, 204, 211, 213, 220, 232; City Hall, 140; election figures, 140; enrollment, 141; Republican organization, 142
Aldermen, Board of, 211
Aldrich, Nelson, 71
Alfange, Dean, 92, 238
aliens, effect on vote, 52
ALP, see American Labor Party
Amalgamated Clothing Workers, 103, 112, 113, 118, 144
American Federation of Labor, 203
American Labor Party, 12, 46, 57, 61, 62, 76, 85, 90–2, 98, 100–3, 105, 107, 108, 109–11, 113–19, 128, 130, 132, 136, 141, 144, 164, 168, 238; state votes (1936–46), 39
American Legion, 69, 90, 201; effect on votes, 50, 51
American Telephone & Telegraph, 226
anti-Semitism: 1938 campaign, 22; effect on voting, 44, 49, 50
Antonini, Luigi, 103
Appeals, see Court of Appeals
Appellate Division, 150–2, 158, 163, 164
Assembly, 83, 166, 168, 170–6, 180. See also Legislature
Assembly districts, 61, 110
Assemblymen, 158
Associated Industries of N. Y. State, 203

Association of the Bar of the City of N. Y., 30, 212
Association of Towns, 202
Attorney General, 90, 115, 189
Audit and Control Dept., 189
Aurelio, Thomas A., 163

bank-deposit insurance, 18
Banking Dept., 192
banking lobby, 201, 204, 208, 209
bar associations, 30, 155–7, 163, 212, 213
Barkley, Alben W., 68
"Barnes machine," 94
Baumes, Caleb, 238
Bausch & Lomb, 37, 144
Bear Mountain Bridge, 135
Belmont, August, 101
Bennett, John J., Jr., 90–2, 115, 116, 238
Berry, Major George, 105
Bicameral Legislature, 173
"big business," 71
Binghamton, 146
Blaine, James G., 234
Bleakley, William F., 76, 138
"blue ribbon" juries, 30
Blumberg, Hyman, 103, 113
Borah, William E., 13, 60, 61
Boston, 219
Bray, M. William, 88
Breitel, Charles D., 195
Broderick, Thomas E., 76, 80, 143
Bronx, the, 86, 89, 94, 97, 100, 109, 111, 115, 129, 135, 156, 158, 162, 196; Democratic organization, 7, 133, 136; county election figures, 135; enrollment, 135
Brooklyn (Kings County), 56, 94, 97, 100, 109, 111, 114, 125, 128, 132, 156; Democratic Party in, 7, 97, 130–2, 148; voting shift,

i

Index

Brooklyn (*continued*)
11; Democratic purge (1940), 40; Republican Party in, 130–3; election figures, 131; enrollment, 131; District Attorney, 132; Democratic machine, 158
budget: division of, 192; Governor's, 198
Buchalter, Louis (Lepke), 104
Buffalo, 42, 65, 145, 223. *See also* Erie County
building codes, 210, 211
building trades unions, 211
Burlingham, Charles C., 212
business tax, 218
Byrnes, James F., 45

California, 234, 235
campaigns, influence on elections, 234–6
Canarsie, 12
Cannon, "Uncle Joe," 170
Capitol Hill, 83
Cardozo, Albert, 165
Cardozo, Benjamin Nathan, 149, 164
Cashmore, John J., 97, 132, 158
Catholics, 90; voting trends, 43, 44; as force in politics, 45, 46; effect on vote, 51; effect on ticket, 84; Church, 201
Chadbourne, William M., 121
Chandler, A. B. (Happy), 68
Chapman, Alger B., 68
Chelsea, 125
Child Labor Amendment, 201
Christian Front, 49
Churchill, Winston, 234
cigarette tax, 217
CIO, *see* Congress of Industrial Organizations
Citizens Union, 213
City Council, New York City, 48, 49, 118, 211
city court justices, 161
City Fusion Party, 107
City Hall, New York, 96, 97, 118, 126, 127, 161, 202, 204, 211, 213
city voting, 42

civil service, 126; commission, 192, 201; pension, 210
Clark, Champ, 14
Cleveland, Grover, 5, 234
clubhouse loafers, 24
Cohoes, 141
Commerce Dept., 192
Communism, 46, 57, 66
Communists, 98–100, 122, 125, 141; New York, 8; party, 102, 103, 104, 108–15, 117–19; penetration into ALP, 102, 104, 108–15
Comptroller, 189
Coney Island, 130, 234
conference of Governors, 6
Congress, 59, 66, 78, 84, 168, 173, 174, 176
Congress of Industrial Organizations, 46, 112, 114
Congressmen, 158
Conservation Dept., 190
Constitution, state, 153, 157, 159, 166, 193, 217, 219, 220, 223, 225; amendments, 38, 173, 174, 176, 179, 181
constitutional convention, 220; of 1938, 76, 208, 209, 210
contributions, 66, 67, 68, 116
Coolidge, Calvin, 73, 237
Copeland, Royal S., 108
Cornell University, 84
Corning, Erastus, 2nd, 140
corporation taxes, 218
Correction Dept., 191
Costello, Frank, 163
counsel, Governor's, 195
counties, 65
County Board of Supervisors, 138
county chairmen, 71, 90, 174, 175, 179, 213
county committees, 62, 100, 118; Democratic, 54–6, 61, 63
county courts, 151, 152, 161
county executives, 138
county leaders, 76, 170
Court of Appeals, 64, 150, 152, 157, 158, 161, 164; nomination to, 161
Court of Claims, 152

Index

Court of Special Sessions, 151, 152

Cox, James M., 94, 237; on Roosevelt ticket, 15

Crane, Murray, 71

Crater, Joseph Force, 159

Crews, John R., 133

Croker, Richard, 44

Curran, Thomas J., 84

Curry, John F., 21, 127, 129, 131, 160

Czechs, voting trends, 47

Daily Worker, 110

Daly, Mark, 203

Davis, John W., 5, 237

death watch, 199

Delaney, John H., 231

delegates, national conventions, 60

Democratic Party, 57, 64, 72, 75, 81, 91, 92, 102, 103, 105, 106, 113–15, 117, 119, 122, 124, 128, 130, 157, 237–9; domination of, 12; national convention, 14, 67; state split (1942), 32; and Dewey, 33; state vote (1936–46), 39; effect of alliances, 46; machinery, 92, 93; control of state, 94; in N.Y.C., 94–7, 99; in N. Y. County, 130; Brooklyn organization, 132; in N.Y.C. suburbs, 139; up-state, 143; in Rochester, 144; Erie County organization, 145; rural vote, 146; and Legislature, 166–85

departments of state government, 188–93

depression, political effect, 16, 17, 18, 36, 73, 74

Dewey, Thomas E., 5, 6, 13, 22, 27, 30–5, 48, 52, 61, 68, 75–84, 87–9, 91–3, 102, 114, 117, 129, 138–40, 142, 163, 177, 182, 187–9, 194–9, 205, 218, 223, 228–30, 238, 239; campaign for district attorney, 29; gang-busting, 30; publicity build-up, 31, 32; renomination for Governor (1942), 32; boss of state,

Dewey, Thomas E. (*continued*) 32, 35; campaign of 1946, 33, 34; presidential nomination (1944), 34, 35; re-election as Governor, 93

discrimination, state commission on, 192–3

district attorneys, 95, 130, 194, 195; Dewey election, 31; New York County, 163, 238; Albany County, 182

district captains, 65, 123

district leaders, 62, 65, 123, 127, 159, 170

Donovan, William J., 84

Dooling, James J., 127

Drum, Hugh A., 84

Dubinsky, David, 103, 104, 110, 112, 113, 115, 116, 118

Dunn survey, 229

Dunnigan, John J., 171

Dutch, the, 140

Dutchess County, 58, 80, 147

Eagle St., Albany, 187

Eastman, George, 143

Eastman Kodak, 37, 143, 144

economic conditions, factor in voting, 50, 53

Education Dept., 190

election: intelligence displayed, 37–9; laws, 55–7, 65, 85, 100, 225; districts, 56, 61, 63; betting, 225, 226; calendar for N. Y. State, 237–9

Elections, Board of, 63–5

Elks, 69

employees of state, effect on vote, 51

English ancestry, 47

enrollment, 58, 59, 62, 108

Erie County, 76, 80, 145; 1928 deal, 16; enrollment, 144; election figures, 145

Estimate, Board of, 205

Executive Dept., 189, 192

Executive Office, 84

Executive Mansion, 187, 188

Family Court, 152

Farley, James A., 32, 33, 87–90,

Farley, James A. (*continued*)
91, 92, 97, 105, 107, 115, 133, 223
Farm Bureau, 82
farm vote, 82
"Fascist" charges, 91
federal employees, 67, 68
Federal Trade Commission, 70
Feinberg, Benjamin F., 84
Finance Committee, Senate, 180
Fish, Hamilton, 58
Fish, Magistrate Lawrence C., 148
five-cent fare, 72
Flynn, Edward J., 44, 47, 89, 97, 105, 107, 115, 133, 135, 158, 211
Foley, James A., 10, 72, 95, 160
Forrestal, James, 45
Fort Orange Club, 203
Fortune, 230
Franco, 90
"full dinner-pail," 73
Fulton County, 167
fur industry, 104
fusion administration, N.Y.C., 205

Gallup poll, 228, 229, 230, 233
Gannett, Frank E., 144
Garibaldi, 73
garment trades unions, 103, 104, 109, 116
Gerlach, Herbert C., 139
German vote, 145; for Wilson, 43
Gimbels, 112
Goldstein, Jonah J., 28, 44, 117, 118, 128, 129, 239
Gompers, Samuel, 105
GOP, *see* Republican Party
governmental regulation, growth of, 8, 9
Governor, 71, 186–99; nomination of, 60; term of office, 170; power of veto, 173, 182, 183, 194; control of Legislature, 178, 179, 188, 189, 193; powers, 194; elections for, 237–9
Governorship, stepping-stone to Presidency, 5, 6

Gracie Mansion, 188
Grand Central, 202
grand jury, run-away, 30
Greeks, voting trend, 47, 48
Greeley, Horace, 5
Green Island, 141
Gridiron Club, 77
gubernatorial convention: of 1932, 20; of 1942, 91
Gunther, John, 201

Hagerty, James A., 195, 231
Hagerty, James C., 195
Hague, Frank, 7, 211
Hamilton County, 167
Hanley, Joe R., 83, 84, 173
Harding, Warren G., 73, 93, 168, 237
Harlem, 98, 99, 122
Harman, John N., 41
Hatch Act, 66, 67
Health Dept., state, 191
Hearst, William Randolph, 95, 108, 122
Heck, Oswald D., 83, 84, 173
Hill, William H., 146
Hilles, Charles D., 71, 76
Hillman, Sidney, 103, 105, 110, 112, 113, 116, 118
Hines, James J., 7
Hiscock, Frank H., 149
Hitler, Adolf, 113
Hitlerism, 47; effect on voting, 44, 47
Hitler-Stalin pact, effect on vote, 110
Hofstadter legislative committee, *see* Seabury investigation
Holland Tunnel, 128, 135
Home Owners' Corp., 18
home relief, 18
home rule, 216–24; amendment, 221, 222; commission, 220
Hoover, Herbert, 15, 17, 36, 73, 74, 76, 138, 168, 231, 237
housing, public, 209
housing division, 192
Howe, Louis McHenry, 15
Hudson River, 135
Hudson River Valley counties, 81, 147

Index

Hughes, Charles Evans, 3, 5, 62, 71, 77, 181, 225, 234, 235
Hylan, John F., 94, 95, 134, 188, 237

immigration, effect on vote, 52, 123
income tax, judicial exemption, 209
Independent Progressive Party, 39
independent vote, 102, 107
industrial belt, voting trend, 41
industrial commissioner, 190
Industrial Government Party, 57
inflation, effect on voting, 48, 50
insurance companies, 171
Insurance Depart., 192
International Ladies Garment Workers Union, 103, 112, 118
Irish, 127, 135, 139; voting trends, 42–6, 48
Irish Catholics, 132; deal with Communists, 98
Italians, 73, 127, 135; racial voting, 46, 47
Ives, Irving M., 83–5, 177, 239

Jackson, Robert, 87
Jaeckle, Edwin F., 76, 85, 145
Jews, 117, 118, 135; voting trends, 43, 44, 46; effect on vote, 51
Johnson, Hiram, 234, 235
judges: nomination of, 60; bipartisan endorsement of, 162–4
judgeship: selling of, 126; purchase of nomination, 154–6
judicial district convention, 60
judicial system, state, 148–64

Kansas, 234; comparison with N. Y., 9
Kansas City, 122
Kean, Hamilton, 71
Keeler's, 23
Kelly, Frank V., 97, 131, 132, 158
Kelly, John, 44
Kennedy, Michael J., Jr., 127
King, Clarence H., 76

Kings County, legislative representation, 167. *See also* Brooklyn
Kiwanis, 69
Knewitz, John J., 136
Know-Nothing movement, 43
Knudsen, William, 112
Koenig, Samuel S., 129
Kracke, Frederick J. H., 132
Ku Klux Klan, 43

labor, 142, 201
Labor and Industrial Relations, School of, 84
Labor Depart., 190
Labor Relations Act, 83
Labor's Non-Partisan League, 105
La Follette, Robert, 8, 237
La Guardia, Fiorello H., 13, 22–8, 31, 37, 44, 47, 75, 76, 89, 96–8, 105–8, 115, 120, 121, 126, 127, 129, 131, 133, 135, 150, 160, 161, 187, 205, 212, 213, 217, 235, 237, 238; as Congressman, 23; as Mayor, 24; reforms, 25, 26; personality, 26, 27; re-election (1937–41), 26; friendship with Roosevelt, 27; Director of Civilian Defense, 28
Landon, Alf M., 9, 61, 226, 229, 234, 238
Law Dept., 189
Lazarus, Reuben A., 220–2
League of Women Voters, 213
legislative correspondents, 79, 86
legislative corruption, 181
legislative leadership, 74, 77, 83, 84, 93, 169, 170, 175, 179, 181, 207; reapportionment, 157, 184
Legislature, 14, 38, 57, 59, 71, 75, 76, 84, 100, 122, 138, 164, 166–85, 190, 193–5, 198, 200, 202, 204, 205, 207, 210, 216–24, 238; Republican control of, 168, 169, 171, 177, 178
Lehman, Herbert H., 13, 15, 19, 21–3, 27, 30–2, 40, 44, 85–92, 96, 101, 105, 114, 115, 124, 131,

Lehman, Herbert H. *(continued)* 150, 169, 170, 188, 189, 194, 195, 197, 199, 206, 217, 230, 235, 237–9; contribution to Smith's campaign, 19; elected Lieutenant Governor, 20; nominated for U.S. Senate, 21; record as Governor, 22, 23; re-elected Governor, 21

Lehman, Irving, 20

Lepke, *see* Buchalter, Louis

Lewis, John L., 105

Lewis County, 110, 174, 175

Liberal Party, 12, 28, 57, 61, 76, 85, 101, 102, 113–15, 117, 119, 128, 132, 144, 238; state votes (1944–6), 39; formation of, 112

Liberty League, 11

licensing, state, 190

Lieutenant Governor, 199; election for, 238

Lippmann, Walter, 17

liquor tax, 218

Literary Digest, 226, 227, 228, 233

"Little Flower," *see* La Guardia, Fiorello H.

Little Green House, 73

Little New Deal, 206

lobbyists, 171, 200–15

Long, Huey, 13

Long Beach, 139

Long Island, 136

Loughlin, Edward V., 127

Luciano, Lucky (Charley Lucky), 7, 31

MacAffer, Kenneth S., 142

Machold, H. Edmund, 70, 71, 231

Macy, W. Kingsland, 25, 74

Macy's, 112

Madison Square Garden, 54, 55

magistrates, 97, 161; courts, 126, 151, 152, 156

Mahoney, Jeremiah T., 108, 238

Mailler, Lee B., 84

majority leader, Assembly, 177

majority leader, Senate, 175

Maine, 226

Manhattan, 61, 111, 114, 122, 125, 128, 135, 154, 157, 162. *See also* New York County

Manton, Martin T., 156

Marcantonio, Vito, 11, 98, 100, 126, 127

Marshall, George C., 28

Marvin, Rolland B., 76, 142

Massachusetts, 219

mayoralty convention of 1933, 24

Mayor, City of N. Y., 237, 238; appointment of judges, 161; relation with state, 222

Mayors, State Conference of, 202

McCarren, Patrick H., 44

McCooey, John H., 94, 95, 125, 130, 131, 158

McGinnies, Joseph A., 74

McGoldrick, Joseph D., 75

McKane, John Y., 44, 130, 234

McKee, Joseph V., 135, 238

McKinley, William, 73

McNett, Charles A., 142

McWilliams, Joe, 49, 52

Mead, James A., 41, 91, 113, 116, 145, 239

Medalie, George Z., 30

Mental Hygiene Dept., 191

message, Governor's annual, 198

militia, state, 192

Miller, Nathan L., 237

millinery workers, 103

Mills, Ogden L., 74, 237

minority leader, Assembly, 177

minor offices, voting for, 39, 40

minor parties, 102, 113, 118, 121; effect of, 12

Mitchel, John Purroy, 212

Moffat, Abbot Low, 83, 84

Monroe County, 76, 143; election figures, 144; enrollment, 144

Morgan, J. P., & Co., 5, 204, 205

Morgenthau, Henry, Jr., 101

Morris, Newbold, 28, 75, 128, 129, 131, 135, 239

mortgage moratorium, 206, 207

Moses, Robert, 27, 168, 134, 238

Motor Vehicle Bureau, 189

Motor Vehicle Commissioner, 88

Index

motor-vehicle tax, 218
mugwumps, 12
municipal courts, 151; justices, 161
municipal elections, 222, 223
municipalities, 216–24
Murphy, Charles Francis, 10, 14, 44, 72, 94, 129, 139, 160

Nassau County, 76, 81, 136, 138, 139; election figures, 137; enrollment, 137
Nast, Thomas, 7
national conventions, 7, 60
nationalities, effect on voting, 46, 47. *See also* racial background
Neal, Clarence H., 98, 99, 127
Nebraska, 173
needle-trades industry, 103
Negroes, 73, 99; vote, 48, 49
Nelson, Donald, 112
New Deal, 16, 18, 73, 92, 93, 107, 123, 131; effect on voters, 46; in N. Y., 23; opposition to within Democratic Party, 103; popularity of, 18; votes in city, 43
New Jersey, 135; judiciary, 149
Newspaper Guild of N. Y., 111
newspaper lobby, 202
newspapers, 195–7; legal advertising, 160
New York City, 54, 58, 62, 63, 65, 72, 73, 81, 92, 94, 109, 110, 114, 124, 136–8, 145, 187, 191, 205, 212, 217, 220, 224, 227, 231, 235; mayoralty: (1925), 95; (1933), 135; (1937), 106; (1945), 28, 129; voting trend, 42; City Council, 48, 49, 98, 118; corruption, 95; Democrats regain control, 97; police department, 121; judiciary, 151–3, 156; charter, 157; legislative representation, 167; legislative measures, 183
New York County, 56, 61, 75, 77, 129, 134, 223; election of 1933, 95; Communist control of ALP, 109; enrollment,

New York County (*continued*) 128; votes and elections, 128; legislative representation, 167. *See also* Manhattan
New York Daily News poll, 230, 231
New York State: electoral vote, 4; size and scope, 4; home of presidential nominees, 5; scope of government, 9; renovation of government, 11; election calendar, 237–9
New York Times, 88, 195, 231
Niagara Falls, 209
Niagara Hudson Power Corp., 70, 71
Norris, George W., 13

O'Brien, John P., 24, 55, 238
O'Connells of Albany, the, 73, 88, 94, 115, 142, 158, 182, 232; machine, 37, 45, 139, 140, 141; Ed, 141; Dan, 141
O'Dwyer, William, 28, 96, 98, 99, 117, 127, 128, 132, 235
"Old Guard," 14, 71, 72, 74, 75, 78, 83, 111
Office of Strategic Services, 84
Ohio, 73
Onondaga County, 76; election figures, 143; enrollment figures, 143
Orange County, 147
organized groups, effect on votes, 50, 51
O'Ryan, John F., 25
Ossining, 177
Ottinger, Albert, 16, 44

PAC, *see* Political Action Committee
Palestine, 211, 233; effect on voting, 44, 48
parent-teacher associations, 201
Park Central Hotel, 104
Parker, Alton B., 5
Parks, State Council of, 190
parole board, 192
parties, organization of, 56, 61, 63

patronage, 116, 117, 126, 158, 159; power, 61, 62, 66; judicial, 149–55, 158, 160
paving-block scandal, 86, 89, 133
Payne, Lou, 81–3
Peck, David W., 163
Pennsylvania, 227, 228
Penn Yan, 12
Perkins, Frances, 10
petitions, 63–5; nominating, 57, 58; primary, 63
Philadelphia, 228
Pitcher, Perley A., 83
Pittsburgh, 228
Platt, Livingston, 139
Poletti, Charles, 45, 47, 92, 199
police justices, 151, 152
Polish voting trends, 47, 48, 145
Political Action Committee, 46, 112, 114
political machines, 120–47
polls, 226–34
population, effect on vote, 52; trends, 81
Potofsky, Jacob, 103
Poughkeepsie, 147
Pound, Cuthbert W., 149
Pratt, Ruth Baker, 74
President of United States, 178, 186; election of 1916, 3; nomination of, 60; elections for, 67, 100, 237, 238; appointment power, 156
press conferences, 195–8
Pressmen's Union, 105
primaries, 55, 57, 59, 60–2, 100, 108, 109, 118; law, 62; control of, 109; elections, 122; nomination of judges, 161
Progressive Party, 234, 235, 237
prohibition, 72, 73, 93
proportional representation, 48, 49, 64, 98, 118
"prosperity," 73
Protestants, voting, 45, 132
Public Service Commission, 88, 191
Public Service Committee of Senate, 70

public utilities, 5, 70, 74, 139, 191, 192, 202, 209; tax, 217, 218
Public Works Dept., 190
Puerto Ricans, 99, 122

Queens, 41, 88, 94, 97, 111, 129, 207

racial background, effect on voting, 43, 44, 47, 48, 49
racing tax, 218
rackets, 29, 88, 95, 104, 120, 132, 135, 196
railroad lobbies, 202
real-estate tax, 217, 218
Regents, Board of, 190, 191
registration, 58, 59, 108
religion, effect on votes, 15, 36, 43–6, 48–50
rent control, 208; law, 35
Representative at Large, 1938 vote, 103
Republican Party, 57, 64, 66, 70–6, 80–3, 85, 92, 102, 103, 107–9, 114, 117, 118, 122, 124, 128, 139, 222, 237–9; control of party, 12, 71, 72; 1910 split, 14; city convention (1933), 25; national conventions, 31, 67, 78, 79; state votes (1936–46), 39; control of state, 93; in N.Y.C., 99; in N. Y. County, 129, 130; Brooklyn organization, 132, 133; Bronx organization, 135; Erie organization, 145; rural vote, 146; and Legislature, 166–85
Richmond, 41, 94
Rochester, 37, 42, 110, 143, 144; state convention, 87
Roosevelt, Eleanor, 105
Roosevelt, Franklin D., 5, 6, 10, 11, 13–20, 22, 23, 27, 28, 32, 40, 45, 47, 48, 53, 54, 82, 84, 86, 87, 89–94, 96, 101, 102, 104–6, 111–17, 119, 123, 124, 130–4, 139, 140, 143, 145, 147, 150, 169, 189, 197, 199, 205, 206, 223, 227–30, 232, 234, 237, 238; 1920 Vice-Presidential nominee, 14, 15; Assistant

Roosevelt, Franklin D. (*cont.*)
Secretary of Navy, 14; path to power, 14–19
Roosevelt, Theodore, 5, 14, 71, 235
Roosevelt, Theodore, Jr., 237
Roper poll, 230
Rose, Alex, 103, 110, 112, 115, 116
Rothstein, Arnold, 104
Rules Committee, Assembly, 175, 176, 182
rural vote, 42, 82, 145, 146
Russia, effect on vote, 46, 98, 114
Ryan, Daniel L., 231
Ryan, Thomas Fortune, 101

St. Lawrence River counties, 70, 146
St. Lawrence seaway project, 147
sales tax, 217
Sampson, Frank J., 100, 127
Saratoga Convention (1942), 79
savings-bank insurance, 170, 171
Schuyler County, 110
Scotch, as voters, the, 47
Scottoriggio, Joseph, 99, 122
Seabury, Samuel, 25
Seabury investigation, 24, 95, 138, 223, 224
Second Assembly District, Brooklyn, 110
Secretary of State, 134
secretary to the Governor, 195
Security and Exchange Commission, 18
Senate, state, 167, 168, 170–4, 176, 180, 184. *See also* Legislature
Senate, U. S., 239; 1946 nomination, 84, 85
Seymour, Horatio, 5
Shapiro, Jacob (Gurrah), 104
"silk-stocking" district, 130
Simpson, Kenneth F., 129, 138
Sing Sing, 199
Smith, Alfred E., 5, 10, 11, 13, 15, 16, 19–22, 32, 36, 38, 71, 72, 86, 90, 93–5, 101, 124, 130, 134, 140, 160, 168, 181, 187, 188, 189, 231, 237

Sobel, Nathan R., 195
Social Security, 18
Social Welfare Dept., 191; State Board of, 191
Socialist Party, 57, 102, 103, 106
soldier vote, 52, 58
Solomon, Charles, 103
"southern tier" counties, 232
speaker, Assembly, 175, 176
special sessions, justices of, 161
Splain, John, 88
Sprague, J. Russel, 76, 80, 138
Stalin, Joseph, 113, 234
Stassen, Harold E., 61
Stand, Bert, 98, 99, 127
state committees, 56, 61; ALP, 110
state convention, 60; delegates, 79
State, Dept. of, 189
State Federation of Labor, 203
State Guard, 84
State Liquor Authority, 192
State Tax Commission, 68
Steingut, Irwin, 177
Stephens, Mallory, 84
Stimson, Henry L., 28
Stone, Horace, 142
suburban counties, 81, 136–9
Suffolk County, 74, 80, 136, 139
Sullivan, Christie, 127
Supreme Court, state, 149–164; secretaries to, 159
Supreme Court, United States, 149, 150, 157, 164
surrogates, 152, 153, 161; New York County, 160
Syracuse, 12, 42, 80, 142, 143, 223

Taber, John, 11
Taft, Robert A., 31
Taft, William H., 14
Taft-Hartley Law, 211, 233
Tammany, 7, 11, 14, 20, 21, 25, 29, 43–5, 54–6, 62, 72, 73, 94–100, 107, 108, 109, 117, 120, 121, 123, 125–9, 131, 132, 134, 139, 150, 156, 160, 164, 195, 231

Taxation and Finance, Dept. of, 189
taxes, 217, 218; state distribution of, 218, 219; local, 223
teachers' lobby, 201
Teapot Dome, 73
Thacher, John Boyd, 140
Thayer, Warren T., 70, 71, 74
"third-term issue," 232, 233
Tilden, Samuel, 5
Tito, Marshal, 99
Tremaine, Morris S., 115
Triangle fire, 10
Troy, 41, 42
Truman, Harry S., 47, 112, 136, 211; doctrine, 100
Tuttle, Charles H., 238
Tweed, William M., 7, 11, 165

Ulster County, 147
unemployment insurance, 190
unions, 102–19 *passim*
University of the State of N. Y., 190
University of Rochester, 144
up-state counties, 110, 227
up-state voting trends, 40, 41
USO (United Service Organization), 88
Utica, 41, 42, 88
Utilities, *see* public utilities

Vermont, 226
voters, 37, 38
votes in state (1936–1946), 39
voting: negative trends, 36, 37; positive, 36, 37; selective 36–8; qualifications for, 38; rural, 42; influenced by nationality, 42–4; machine, 66, 85

Wadsworth, James W., 85
Wagner, Robert F., 10, 72, 84, 160

Wagner Labor Relations Act, 211
Waldman, Louis, 103
Walker, James J., 10, 20, 24, 26, 43, 54, 55, 72, 95, 96, 116, 124, 134, 160, 188, 223, 224, 237, 238
Wall Street, 5
Wallace, Henry A., 47, 100, 112, 118
Ward, Hamilton, 16
Ward, William L., 138
Washington, D. C., 66, 200, 207, 211
Waterman, Frank D., 237
Watertown, 146
Ways and Means Committee, Assembly, 180
Welsh, as voters, the, 47
Westchester, 76, 80, 81, 136, 138, 139, 177; enrollment, 137; election figures, 137
Whitman, Charles S., 93, 237
Willkie, Wendell L., 5, 18, 31, 40, 77–80, 140, 142, 228, 229, 232, 233, 238
Wilson, Woodrow, 3, 14, 43, 156, 225
Wilson-Pakula Law, 100, 118
Wisconsin, 59
women, effect on vote, 52
Workers' Party, 57
Workmen's Compensation, 190
World War II, effect on electorate, 229
WPA (Work Projects Administration), 68, 124, 229

Yonkers, 12, 139
Yorkville, 49
Young, Fred, 174, 175
Young, Owen D., 89, 92

Zionists, effect on voting, 44

A NOTE ON THE TYPE

IN WHICH THIS BOOK IS SET

The text of this book has been set on the Linotype in a type-face called "Baskerville." The face is a facsimile reproduction of types cast from molds made for John Baskerville (1706–1775) from his designs. The punches for the revived Linotype Baskerville were cut under the supervision of the English printer George W. Jones.

John Baskerville's original face was one of the fore-runners of the type-style known as "modern face" to printers: a "modern" of the period A.D. 1800.

The book was composed, printed, and bound by Kingsport Press, Inc., Kingsport, Tennessee.